The Sovereigntist's Handbook

Charting the course to western independence

Greymor Ventures Ltd., Calgary, Alberta, Canada
corymorgan.com

ISBN 978-1-7388110-0-7
Cover image created by Lyle Krahn krahnicles.com
Copy editor, Amanda Brown at Blue Pencil Solutions
Formatting, the longsuffering Jane Morgan

Printed in Canada

In memory of Brian (Hutch) Hutchinson
For all the barstool inspiration as we solved
the world's problems together.

INTRODUCTION

It happens every few years. Politicians in Ottawa marginalize Western Canada for their own political benefit, Westerners become furious, independence movements blossom, then they fade away. It's a cycle as certain as the seasons and it must be broken.

At the time of writing, there are several independence-minded groups and political parties in the west of the country. In Alberta alone there are four registered independence-leaning political parties.

The Advantage Party of Alberta garnered 0.3 percent of the vote in the 2015 general election.

There's the Buffalo Party of Alberta, which has never fielded a candidate in an election. The Independence Party of Alberta collected a staggering twenty-four votes in a 2022 by-election in Fort McMurray and whose leader is now controversial street preacher, Artur Pawlowski. The Wildrose Independence Party had a showing of 11 percent in the 2022 by-election in Fort McMurray but now is wracked with infighting and has two leaders and two boards battling it out against one another in the courts while the party withers.

While support for independence in Alberta sits at a solid 25 percent, no independence party has managed to turn that base of support into a lasting or effective entity.

As far as non-partisan independence groups go, they form and disappear even faster than political parties. Independence advocates need to re-examine how they are doing things.

Why do these parties and movements continue to fail when there is such a strong base of support for the concept?

Part of the reason lies in the nature of independence supporters. Typically, supporters of independence are individualists who have little use for or trust in authority or central leadership. Can you think of a demographic any harder to try and organize? —Talk about herding cats.

Proponents of western independence need to stop looking to groups and parties to provide the path to independence—this isn't going to work. Political parties are a part of the puzzle, but they will only react to growing support for independence, they can't create it. Likewise, while think tanks and advocacy groups can contribute to building support for independence, they don't have the staying power and can't build the political clout to push the ball past the goal line.

Bringing the West to independence will lie with the individual.

A true grassroots foundation for independence must be created, then the politicians will follow. Individuals must build the base. Supporters for independence should realize there will be no messiah or organization that will create widespread support for the concept. The task for creating a lasting and ultimately effective base of support for independence lands in our own laps. Nobody else is going to do it for us.

Supporters already know where we need to go. Now they must re-evaluate how to get there.

The purpose of this book isn't to make you a supporter for independence—I assume you're already there, or at least close. This book aims to teach you how to become an effective advocate for independence so you can bring others into the fold. If we can't get individuals to work as a group for a common goal, we must look at building a base of the population to work as individuals, independently and separately for the common goal.

An effective advocate for independence needs faculty; they must have communication skills both in person and on social media, they should have ready answers to common questions about independence, a solid grounding in western history, and a working knowledge of current political party structures and how to work effectively within them.

The aim of the following chapters is to transform the reader from a frustrated citizen into an effective individual advocate for independence.

Independence movements in the West have come and gone several times since the 1980s. They keep following the same pattern of rising fast and flaring out. It seems impossible for any organization—

whether in the form of a party or activist group—to create a long-lasting entity. It's because we keep repeating the same mistakes.

We know where we want to go but always get lost along the way. Much of the reason for this is that no one had written a handbook.

I still don't know it all, by any means, but with twenty years of political experience now under my belt, I know a hell of a lot more now than I did when I stumbled through the leadership of the Alberta Independence Party (AIP.) I can't help but think that it might have ended differently if I and the other key organizers had some sort of instruction manual created by someone with substantial and relevant experience. We still may not have brought the West to independence by this point, but we might have set in place a lasting foundation for the movement.

With guidance, we could have communicated our message more effectively. We might have better managed our volunteers, organized our structures more effectively, and drawn new supporters to the cause. We might also have created an enduring nonpartisan movement.

Independence initiatives are forming and burning out every year now. The support for western independence is stronger than ever and yet the movement still gets stuck in a cycle of rising, cresting, treading water and then self-destructing. The cycle must be broken if western independence is ever to become a real possibility.

Look at support for western independence as a wave coming in from the ocean and receding with the tide. Instead of allowing that body of water to retreat after the wave breaks, we must capture and embrace it to buoy us up for the next wave. We need to consolidate support when the wave is high and sustain it when the tide goes out. This way, permanent and lasting support for independence will slowly but surely build.

Parties, think tanks, and activist groups will always play a role, but they can't get the job done alone. Western independence must be cultivated in true grassroots fashion, person by person. We build the foundation of the movement with thousands, then millions of people rather than a handful of small groups representing those proponents. Every one of us is responsible for building that groundswell and keeping our eye on the collective goal instead of becoming lost in the organizations that pursue it.

I've spent years thinking about past efforts while working on contemporary strategy. I want to share what I've learned so you can take advantage of the road already travelled.

Why listen to me? Because I've been there and done that. If the movement is to continue to make errors, let's ensure they are new ones. Eventually the formula for a successful independence movement will emerge.

There are many books on western independence. Some are opposed to it, some are in support, and some tell its history. None offer advice on how to get to western independence.

We need a guide and a plan.

Chapter 1

A HISTORY OF THE WESTERN INDEPENDENCE MOVEMENT IN ALBERTA—MY STORY

So, who is Cory Morgan and why should anybody listen to him?

I will share with you some of my own background and why I have both positive and negative experiences from which to draw for the purposes of this book. If we don't learn from and document our errors, we will be bound to repeat them. I assure you I've made plenty of mistakes. They need to be shared to be useful examples of how *not* to do something.

I have always been a political wonk. I am not sure why. I remember watching the news even before I was a teenager and barraging my parents with questions about issues and people. I ravenously consumed books and newspapers while I was growing up. At the same time, my peers were focused on sports and music. I did my fair share of partying and taking part in questionable activities in my youth, however, I always retreated to current affairs and political reading when I was alone.

I joined the Reform Party when I was twenty years old and volunteered for them at every opportunity. I was fascinated with elected officials and how their campaigns and networks operated. I was a young man in a party overrepresented by grey-haired folks, I found myself invited to many events and campaigns. It wasn't because I was a brilliant campaigner with experience to lend, invitations came because the party desperately needed to project an image of youth involvement. For event photos, I was often positioned in the background alongside other young conservatives to try to hide the reality that the average age of an attendee at a Reform Party event was sixty, or older.

I became involved with the Alberta Party in my mid-twenties and for a couple of years served on its provincial board. The party was tiny and hadn't fielded a candidate in an election in years. My experience was still valuable since I learned how party committees and executive boards functioned, what a party constitution entailed, and how a party operates more generally within a local legislative environment.

In the year 2000, regional tensions in Canada were growing. Five years prior in a 1995 referendum, Quebec had come within a mere one-percent margin of gaining independence. In response to this, and with renewed purpose, the Chrétien Liberals focused more intensely on creating policies that benefitted Central Canada at the expense of the country's outlier provinces. The West was treated as a piggy bank and raided regularly by the Liberals to buy Quebec's love through transfer payments. When we in the West protested, we were either ignored or scorned as rednecks who couldn't appreciate what Confederation was doing for us.

After more than a decade of failed efforts and ongoing compromise, the Western-Canadian-focused Reform Party dissolved and it became the Canadian Alliance. Many of us believed our time and effort with the Reform Party had been wasted. We were dejected. We had no interest in going back to what we thought would be just another version of the Progressive Conservative Party, which at best would be less hostile to western interests than the Liberals had been.

I concluded that further efforts to achieve change beneficial for the West in terms of federation would be futile as had several of my compatriots from the parties I was involved in. The Canadian system was broken. Nothing we could do within the current set of political rules would lead to any meaningful change for the West.

It was time to think outside the box and that meant the focused pursuit of independence for Western Canada.

There was no functional western independence party at that time. The Western Canada Concept—a secessionist political party founded in 1980—was still active at a federal level and within BC under Doug Christie's leadership, but there was no organized presence in Alberta.

In finding no partisan options to join, I decided to get to work on forming a new one. How hard could it be? A few of us broke away from the Alberta Party and got to work on building the Alberta Independence Party (AIP).

Most of us were in our twenties, so of course, we thought we knew it all. One of our first orders of business was to build a website for the party. Indeed, in some ways we were ahead of our time, few political parties had websites. That aside, we really didn't know what the hell to do. We held small meetings and tried to gather supporters via the internet. We floundered for a few months.

By the fall of 2000, we had perhaps one hundred members only a couple dozen of who were active. We needed thousands of signatures for an official government petition to become a registered political party and we were spinning our wheels. We knew what we wanted, but just couldn't figure out how to achieve it.

One of the obstacles we faced was many of the people we'd assumed would come aboard still hung onto hope for change on the federal front. They believed the Canadian Alliance Party (CAP) could win a federal election and would address western grievances upon achieving power. They just weren't ready to embrace independence yet. Independence-minded organizers deal with this same misplaced optimism every federal election cycle.

Things took a different turn for us when then prime minister Jean Chrétien called an early snap election in late October 2000. The campaign was heated and vitriol was continually directed at Western Canada.

Chrétien used regional division as a deliberate strategy. He only spent nine days in Western Canada during the campaign with a mere two in Alberta. Chrétien openly stated in an interview he didn't like dealing with Westerners. He didn't make any secret of his contempt for the region. This approach by Chrétien was considered and purposeful. He had taken part in just such a campaign in the past.

In 1980, former prime minister Pierre Trudeau embarked on a similarly divisive election campaign. Liberal campaign organizer Keith Davey laid out the party strategy stating unapologetically, "Screw the West. We'll take the rest!" Trudeau won a majority in that campaign. So far, regional divisiveness at the expense of the West has always paid off for the Liberal party.

Chrétien's tactic of inflaming regional division in the 2000 election was no less successful than Trudeau's had been. By election day in mid-November, the Liberal Party was virtually shut out of Western Canada yet still managed to increase its majority by eleven seats. It became crystal clear Western Canada was considered irrelevant in federal politics.

Infuriated and frustrated Westerners who had put their faith and support in the CAP were suddenly looking for a new political home. The ranks of the fledgling AIP suddenly began to swell. Many people who had declined their involvement with us just months earlier were now calling and offering to help.

Early 2001, our website caught the eye of a reporter with Canada's *National Post* who wrote a story about us. Virtually overnight our little organization came into the national spotlight and as interim leader I was caught in the middle of it. I was scared out of my wits as I grappled with constant TV and radio appearances and interviews for the print media. I learned how it feels to draw national ridicule as establishment media outlets went out of their way to discredit our organization, the independence movement, and me. The stress was overwhelming.

Although we were not yet a formally registered party, our membership numbers exploded into the thousands as people mailed cash and cheques. We scheduled a founding convention for mid-January in Red Deer to establish and organize some sort of formal structure.

On the day of the convention, we really didn't know what to expect. We didn't have the means for online organization of events then as we do now. We relied on people to show up and register at the door. We had no idea whether dozens of people would show, or thousands. We didn't have a clue.

People arrived by the hundreds. We had constantly to bring extra chairs to accommodate the new arrivals. Eventually it was standing room only for attendees in the venue. It was also terrifying to observe the entire back wall of the room had been taken up with TV cameras and reporters.

With a loose agenda and a day to fill, I kicked off the event with my opening speech. Or at least, I tried to. I stepped up to the podium, peered out over those hundreds of faces watching me in anticipation, and I froze. It was a true deer-in-the-headlights moment. I'd spent days memorizing and planning my speech and I forgot every single word of it. I choked and stared into the room blankly. I swear I have never heard such a deafening silence.

I muttered a few awkward words on how the Clarity Act gave us permission to pursue independence and then fled to my seat as the room offered some awkward, sympathetic applause. I've spoken at many public speaking events since and have thankfully never frozen like that since.

We managed to formally establish a board of directors at the meeting despite our inexperience, and I did recover myself well enough to answer a number of questions from the floor. It's worth noting most of our party directors were under thirty years of age. At one point, we lost control of the agenda when a motion from the floor called for the party to take a soft-independence approach, and it won the room.

Despite our poor planning, for the most part, the convention was a success. We had raised funds, made national news, and established a solid core of organizers.

We desperately needed to become a registered party, though. Without registration, we couldn't offer tax credits for donors, nor could candidates appear on an election ballot under the party brand. As organizers, this was where we learned a hard but valuable lesson.

We thought it would be easy. We needed 6,000 signatures on an official government petition to become registered. We mailed thousands of forms to members with a return envelope and a request to get signatures from family and friends. We figured if even a quarter of those who had purchased memberships got a few signatures and returned them to us, we would have this registration thing out of the way within a week or two.

The key lesson we learned was this: in any volunteer organization, a tiny percentage of people do most of the work. While it was easy to get people to commit to spending ten dollars on a membership, it turned out we were asking too much to get them to petition for us. We gained perhaps 2,000 signatures in the weeks following our mail-out. While internet petitions are easily filled, getting a person to commit a signature along with a phone number and address to a paper form was apparently a bridge too far. Signatories were well short of what we needed. We would have to change tactics.

At the beginning of February 2001, just weeks after our convention, then premier Ralph Klein called an election in Alberta—we were out of time.

The party managed to put together fourteen independent candidates to run. It proved impossible to mount much of a campaign since we'd been handicapped by fundraising restrictions and unable to get the party name onto the ballot. While our candidates fared much better than independent candidates typically do, they barely registered on the electoral radar on the day of the vote.

The public and most of our volunteers lost interest in the AIP after the provincial election. The trickle of incoming petition signatures for party registration dried up as did new memberships and the media coverage. The doldrums had set in. It was difficult to gain any kind of attention, much less gain active participants.

By the end of the summer our little organization was nearly dead. I didn't know what to do and so I stepped aside as leader. A few board members wanted me gone and I was happy to oblige. A handful of organizers worked to keep things active for a while, but it all faded quickly. I don't regret forming the party at all. I see it now as an important step and a great learning experience, even if it was just another flash-in-the-pan party.

The failure of the AIP to become a lasting entity was greatly due to inexperience. I was very much out of my depth as a leader, as were most of our key organizers. We had the optimism and energy of youth, but little of the experience that maturity provides.

I took a couple years off from direct political involvement before my return to the arena. In 2004 I put my name on the ballot with the Separation Party of Alberta (SPA). This was one political move I *do* regret because I did it for the wrong reasons; I was bored and didn't want to sit out an election, so I tossed my hat into the ring for the constituency of Highwood (Southern Alberta). It was hardly an inspired entry into a race. Still, the election taught me more valuable lessons.

I was under no illusions the SPA would win the election, or even a seat. I did think the party would do better than the AIP had done since the SPA wasn't ambiguous about its goals and it was a registered entity. I was dead wrong. The party was slaughtered in every constituency. I think only the Alberta Communist Party did worse on a per-candidate basis. I learned the futility of door knocking while wearing apparel with the word "separation" in the party's name.

People might talk a big game when it comes to independence, but when push comes to shove on a real ballot, they often just won't make that mark. It takes more than an election campaign to create dedicated supporters for independence.

I joined the Alberta Alliance Party (AAP) in 2006. It was a great experience and a wild ride as the party grew from a single-seat rump in the legislature to become the official opposition. The AAP went on to present a serious challenge to the provincial government in the 2012 and 2015 elections. I served in varying capacities from vice president of policy on the provincial executive to managing campaigns. We had ups and downs, electoral wins and losses, and more than a few internal battles. I learned about gains that can be made through the hard work of members and about the catastrophic consequences of politicians' clashing egos. The party morphed into the Wildrose Party then eventually folded into the Progressive Conservatives (PCs) to become what today is the United Conservative Party (UCP) and, of course, the battles continue.

I have finished with direct involvement in party politics though I still follow closely. The role of observer and commentator from an independent media standpoint suits me well.

Chapter 2

THE SYSTEM IS BROKEN

When making the case for independence, it's important to explain how and why the current Canadian system is fundamentally flawed. Those who don't watch politics closely must understand the futility of attempting to accomplish substantial and lasting change within a system that's stacked against them. It's dry subject matter, but it has to be covered. When we realize the system can't be fixed, we become truly dedicated supporters of independence. It will take time to make that case.

Canada isn't the problem. It's the intractable, out-of-date, biased system that's broken. Be sure to always differentiate between the country and its system of governance.

Born this way

Canada's entire political system is imbalanced. It's designed to treat outlying provinces as resource producers to be plundered for the benefit of the centre of the country. Provinces beyond Ontario and

Quebec are not considered partners within Confederation so much as vassal states beholden to Ottawa.

We shouldn't take it personally. The system made sense to the nation's founders when Canada was created. In 1867, the entire population west of the Ontario border made up less than 4 percent of the whole population of Eastern Canada. Why would we have considered such a tiny minority of the population?

Population distribution has changed dramatically in the last 150 years. Western Canada now has around 12.4 million people while Eastern Canada has approximately 25 million. We've grown from 4 percent of Canada's population to nearly 30 percent, but the way we're being governed, you wouldn't know it.

Political systems are usually created with the aim of balancing power regionally, and by population. In the United States for example, every state has two representatives in the Senate no matter its population. The number of Congress representatives sent per state depends on population, however. Nevada has four members of Congress while California has fifty-three.

The American system was born of revolution and thus designed with empowerment of citizens in mind. The Canadian parliamentary system evolved from the monarchical system and while it's democratic by design, the power of the state was intended to be supreme over that of the individual. Canada's motto of "peace, order and good government" reflects this. It's a nice fluffy statement but says nothing about the needs of the individual. Regional differences were of no consideration either. The system was designed in a way that makes change almost impossible.

The American system is far from perfect, but it forces the drafting of legislation to bear a degree of regional interests and needs in mind. While highly populated states dominate Congress, if they tried to pass national legislation that would be punitive to states with smaller populations, the legislation would never pass the Senate. Likewise, smaller states can't ally with one another and pass legislation through the Senate at the expense of the larger states since it wouldn't get through Congress. Some degree of compromise must be sought in order to pass national bills.

Canada has a bicameral system, one that was ostensibly set up to balance population and regional needs, but it's hopelessly dysfunctional. The way the Canadian Senate works is an insult to the concept of regional balance.

Canadian senators are appointed rather than elected. The prime minister selects senators and the seats are generally gifted as rewards for political favours. Broader regional needs are rarely if ever taken into consideration when appointing senators. If anything, senators who've demonstrated support for Central Canada are likely to have acquired their appointments because of their ability to curry favour with the region's voters. They don't want upstart senators to actually do their job and make noise on behalf of the regions they ostensibly represent—that has the potential to make things awkward for the federal party in power. From the viewpoint of most prime ministers, pliable politicians who aren't inclined to rock the boat are ideal selections for the Senate.

While Canadians senators are very well compensated, they have few incentives to be productive. They are appointed until the age of seventy-five and it's almost impossible to expel a senator once they've taken their seat. In 1998, Senator Andrew Thompson enraged the nation with his chronic absenteeism. It was found he'd been residing in Mexico rather than show up for his Senate duties. He'd attended the Senate only forty-seven times in fourteen years and it took months of political pressure before senators sanctioned him. Even then, he was never formally expelled from the Senate. He was suspended at age seventy-three and resigned a month later. Thompson will enjoy a very generous pension for the rest of his life.

Senators can choose to be active in committees and they do occasionally hold productive hearings on various issues. For the most part, senators take a nobody-moves-nobody-gets-hurt approach to their jobs. If they keep their heads down and show up just enough so no one notices their absences, they can make good money and qualify for the kind of pension ordinary Canadians can only dream of.

The Canadian Senate is a joke as far as democratic principles are concerned. It's an even bigger joke as far as regional representation goes. It does nothing to address legislative dominance due to population. The West is grossly underrepresented.

There are 105 senators in Canada. A distribution of ten senators per province—with a few shared by the territories—would make it look something like a Senate intended to balance legislative power among the regions. The distribution looks nothing like that, however.

Right now, Eastern Canada has seventy-eight senators while all the territories and provinces west of Ontario have only twenty-seven. Quebec and Ontario each have twenty-four senators. The Senate is stacked to support neither Canada's regional needs nor its population distribution. It's an institution serving the Laurentian Elite.

The House of Commons will always serve Central Canada's needs simply because most of the nation's population is there. Canada's government doesn't follow the rules governing proportional representation when demographic changes don't favour Quebec.

Cooking the books

The distribution of seats in the House of Commons is revisited and adjusted every few years. In 2022 however, it was found that Quebec had lost population and would lose a seat in Parliament as a result. Alberta stood to gain a few seats due to population growth.

This only makes sense, right?

Wrong!

This travesty surely couldn't stand.

The Bloc Quebecois tabled a motion to modify the seat distribution formula to ensure Quebec never risks losing a seat, again. This isn't surprising. The Bloc stands up for Quebec first and foremost. Western MPs should be paying close attention to their example.

The problem is the Bloc's motion passed easily. Not only with the support of the Liberals and the NDP, but also with that of many Conservative Party of Canada (CPC) MPs. It shows Central Canada's interests will always be considered first, even on an issue as simple as seat distribution. They essentially voted against the math and have admitted we don't have a true system of representation by population. It is and will remain a system of representation through central government serving Central Canada's interests first.

Any party with national aspirations won't hesitate to throw the West under the bus in their pursuit of the love of central Canadian voters—Conservative or Liberal, it just doesn't matter. Many western Conservative party members will abstain rather than take a stance and vote in favour of the West. So, what's the point of local representation when your local MPs won't stand up for you in Parliament? The game is rigged, and we can never win while playing on this field.

Canada's legacy media was virtually silent on the successful motion to abandon fair, representation based on population. Sure, it only means one extra seat for Quebec, but this is a big deal—the precedent has been set. The distribution of seats will remain concentrated in central Canada no matter how populations migrate. There should be media panels discussing and decrying this. There should be headlines shouting about it and columnists rebuking it. Instead, we've heard nothing. This is what happens when the media becomes dependent on federal government bailouts and subsidies. They will never bite the hands that feed them.

Canada's Supreme Court is as imbalanced as the Canadian Senate. The prime minister appoints members, and while they must be competent adjudicators, they're always appointed for political rather than practical reasons. And as we might expect, political interests in Ottawa mean the Supreme Court is slanted in favour of Central Canada. Canada is far from alone in having politically appointed justices in the high court and it should therefore be noted that the West ought not to expect remedy in Canada's top court.

While Quebec makes up less than a quarter of Canada's population, a third of the Supreme Court must comprise judges from Quebec. Another third must come from Ontario (though at least their population warrants it). While Western Canada makes up a third of the nation's population, we will never get more than two of nine spots on the Supreme Court bench. If we want regional grievances addressed by the Supreme Court, right off the bat the odds aren't good.

Paper tigers and rubber stamps

The Governor General is the highest authority in Canada, but let's be realistic, while the role is powerful in theory, its power is only symbolic. The Governor General is appointed by the prime minister and in real terms will always answer to the prime minister. Those appointed to the role of Governor General don't write throne speeches, they just deliver them. They don't create or scrutinize legislation they merely rubber-stamp it. If for some reason a Governor General ever decided to stand up and oppose the will of Parliament, it would spell the end of the constitutional monarchy. Our elected officials would dismantle the office of the Governor General in the blink of an eye. In any case, it simply won't happen—those appointed to office know on which side their bread is buttered and they won't put at risk their role as the nation's highest paid ribbon-cutter.

The symbolic power of the Governor General has inspired several misguided efforts on the part of the people. We had best clear up some apparent misunderstanding.

I have seen groups claim a Governor General can be obligated to remove a prime minister or premier via petition. Let me make it clear: even if you handed the Governor General a petition signed in blood by 90 percent of the Canadian population demanding the removal of an elected official, the Governor General does not have to act upon it, nor would they. It's not in the cards. It's a waste of ink, or blood, or whatever the signatures came in. Quit wasting everyone's time!

A small group taking part in the Freedom Convoy protests of 2022 naively suggested the Governor General could be compelled to overthrow the government. All they managed to accomplish was to hand protest opponents the ammunition they needed to claim the Freedom Convoy protesters were planning an insurrection. This is an example of why every movement has to ensure its fringe supporters are sidelined.

I do understand the appointment of the Governor General, senators, and Supreme Court members is all based on the "recommendation" of the prime minister. In theory, the British monarch appoints members. It's all just pomp and circumstance. The Crown won't dispute any recommendations from the prime minister. If we want a system with real checks and balances, we need to create a new one. Until then, we are under the control of a prime minister with near dictatorial authority.

Some are more equal than others

While the Canadian Senate provides faux regional political balance, the constitutionally entrenched equalization program provides a false economic balance.

The equalization program has challenged Canadian unity since its inception in 1957. It began as a program modelled to address fluctuations in regional prosperity, but quickly morphed into a political tool and an entitlement for Quebec.

While equalization itself is constitutionally entrenched, the formula for it isn't. The program could be readjusted or defunded by Parliament. That of course won't happen. Much like the formula for parliamentary seat distribution, the equalization formula will always be rigged to benefit Central Canada. And again, it doesn't matter which party is in power. Stephen Harper and Jason Kenney were both vociferous critics of the equalization program when they were in opposition roles. Once the CPC formed a majority government, however, it did nothing to reform the program. It would have cost too many precious Quebec and Maritime votes.

While every province west of Manitoba pays into the program, Alberta has been milked the hardest—by a country mile. Alberta collected a few million dollars in equalization at the beginning of the program. Since then, Alberta has always been a net contributor to the program. Despite decades of ups and downs in the western economy, the equalization formula is somehow always adjusted to keep Alberta paying. Even during the early 1980s when Albertans were losing their homes in droves because of the National Energy Program and double-digit interest rates, Alberta still kept paying into the Canadian pool.

In recent energy downturns, Alberta and Saskatchewan have suffered dearly when energy royalties have diminished. Still, they somehow never qualified to receive equalization payments. The formula manages to ensure the West is perpetually drained no matter the state of its economy.

It's hardly a coincidence that Quebec almost always nets the same amount from equalization that Alberta loses. While Quebec's economy is strong, the formula is rigged—unsurprisingly—in their favour. Hydroelectric revenue in Quebec is exempt from equalization calculations, yet *all* western resource revenue is always included. This ensures Quebec will be declared a have-not province in perpetuity and will qualify for transfers. It's akin to making a rich kid's trust fund income exempt so they qualify for welfare payments. Not only does this rip off working people, but it's also a disincentive for the handout recipient to seek other forms of revenue.

Quebec banned oil and gas development and exploration in the province despite them having some potentially lucrative deposits. Much of the reason for the ban is if they develop those resources, the royalties they collect will be deducted from their incoming equalization payments. They prefer to remain dependent on Confederation and continue virtue signalling on the environment by ostensibly banning industries in their own province. Meanwhile they import their oil and gas from other countries such as Saudi Arabia and Venezuela.

Equalization, like other welfare-based programs, acts as a disincentive for the recipient to become self-sufficient. Quebec can afford to refuse oil and gas development in their own province, while sucking revenues from energy-producing provinces. If equalization payments were to be cut off, we would see drilling rigs popping up all over Quebec like spring dandelions. For the same reasons, universal basic income (UBI) schemes are destined to fail.

Supporters of the status quo will always dismiss western complaints about the equalization program as being misguided or selfish. They will say westerners are misinformed and they don't understand the program. It's true that many people do have a misunderstanding of the mechanics of the legislation itself. The program is indeed convoluted and not easily explained. That doesn't mean that opposition to the program is misplaced.

Provinces don't issue direct payments for their contribution to equalization, federal taxes are taken from them then doled out Canada-wide by the federal government via transfers. Equalization is just the most galling, unfair, and odious of the transfer payments. Equalization visibly demonstrates the nation's regional favouritism thus making it a flashpoint for opposition.

Haughty supporters of Canada's interprovincial welfare system love to point out that even if equalization were gone today, provinces wouldn't pay a lesser amount into the federal system. This is true. However, the federal government would have one less program to use to buy regional love. It would have extra funds for other transfers such as those for health care, which could be increased for all provinces. In theory, that would lead to more funds for all provinces previously paying into equalization. That won't happen of course because the federal government will never substantially reform Canada's equalization program, much less scrap it.

Equalization is the most visible way the West is bled of finances by the East. We suffer a fiscal death by a thousand cuts through transfer payments, subsidies, and preferential legislation.

Over the last fifty years, Alberta alone has contributed over $600 billion more into Confederation than it received in return through transfers and services. The picture is similar in other western provinces. Most of it comes through preferential transfers for program spending. The federal government hands out more money to eastern provinces than western ones. Some of the imbalances are less obvious and can't so easily be measured.

The French advantage

The requirements for bilingualism heavily favour the central provinces. The federal government directly employs over 320,000 people. They indirectly employ at least as many more through contracts. Requirements for bilingualism result in huge advantages for bilingual job applicants in Central Canada. For example, only 2 percent of Saskatchewan's population speaks French, which means fewer Saskatchewan citizens pursue or land government jobs in Central Canada. Well-paying government jobs in Western Canada usually have a requirement for French language proficiency despite the number of unilingual French speakers in Canada being negligible.

Bilingual requirements have led to a massive overrepresentation of Quebecers in the federal civil service. Not only does this funnel billions of salary and contract dollars into Central Canada's pockets, it also helps maintain that bias in federal policy—again supporting Central Canada. Politicians come and go, but many of those civil servants are in their government jobs for life. Civil servants arguably have a more direct impact on Canadian policy than elected officials. The transfer of both fiscal and legislative power to Central Canada through the civil service is both hugely significant but almost impossible to quantify. We rarely hear about this imbalance, but it's as real and unfair as equalization.

While not every civil servant needs to speak French, the federal civil service must provide government services in French, regardless of where in the country or how slight the demand for it. Examples are absurd and plentiful. In Saskatchewan, small town post offices were caught between a rock and a hard place as postmasters went into retirement but could only be replaced with bilingual employees. It didn't matter nobody had ever asked for service in French in those towns. The laws were rigid and unforgiving. Towns had to scramble to find a French speaker to move there, or quickly train someone to be fluent in French. Regulations like this have allowed French speakers to dominate the entire federal civil service. Non-French speakers are also at a big disadvantage when it comes to promotions within the civil service.

In April of 2022, the Liberal government tabled Bill C-13 that would apply the same standards of bilingualism to the federally regulated private sector as the public sector. It would impact almost one million employees in Canada.

This would prove an economic windfall for the Québécois as an exporter of French-speaking employees to serve in well-paying jobs in regions where French isn't spoken. Of course it will also pressure businesses to simply set up shop in Quebec where they can access a ready pool of French-speaking employees. It's a very subtle but effective way to shift economic advantage to Quebec and parts of Central Canada. Not every wealth transfer is as overt as equalization.

Young and old

Some of the economic bias is based on demographics.

The Prairie provinces have a younger workforce than Eastern Canada. The median age in Saskatchewan, Alberta, and Manitoba is thirty-eight. In Ontario it's forty-two, Quebec forty-three, and in Newfoundland and Labrador it's forty-eight. Western workers are putting a disproportionate amount of money into the Canada Pension Plan while eastern populations are drawing out more than they put in. This situation is unlikely to be of purposeful, malignant intent, but it's yet another example of how the centralized Canadian system puts the West at an economic disadvantage.

Economically defenseless

The West's inability to defend itself from ideologically driven federal governments has been costly. Beginning in 1980, the National Energy Program drained Alberta in the region of $50–$100 billion in its few short years and left the province in a deep recession. While Albertans were furious, they had no recourse within the Canadian system to stave off the federal assault.

Prime Minister Justin Trudeau's ideological government has been no better. By 2020, the Trudeau administration's anti-energy legislation and regulation has resulted in the cancellation of $150 billion in new projects, from liquid natural gas terminals to oilsands mines. Tanker bans and pipeline cancellations have turned the West into an investment pariah and there's nothing that can be done within the current system to change it. Even if there's a change in government, the western economy will still be too vulnerable to hostile federal powers to make it a safe place to invest.

The Canadian system of transfer payments leaves provinces beholden to the federal government. Traditionally, the federal government dangles those dollars—carrot-and-stick-style—in front of provincial governments.

For example, when Alberta started to expand its medical diagnostic imaging capacity through private MRI clinics in the 1990s, the federal government under Jean Chretien threatened to cut health care transfer payments to Alberta as punishment for its deviation from the Canadian principle of private health care prohibition. While provinces are tasked with managing their own health care systems, they are dependent on federal health care transfer payments to fund them.

While the Canadian Medical Care Act called for the federal government to fund 50 percent of the health care expenses of the provinces, the federal government typically only covers about 25 percent of the health care costs in western provinces. That portion of the health care budget is still enough for the federal government to use as a stick to keep provinces toeing the line.

The federal government uses those kinds of transfer schemes to bully provincial governments into participation in programs they'd rather decline. Alberta didn't want any part of the Trudeau Liberal's national childcare program. The province was forced to embrace it because the federal government would have withheld the funding transfer had the province not implemented its program for them. Money taken from provincial taxpayers would have been given to other regions if the provincial government had rejected the federal scheme.

There is no provincial defense against federal governments using transfer payments as a means of economic blackmail—aside from independence, that is. The system forces federal parties to cater to Central Canadian voters and they use business subsidies to do it.

While western industries must ride out economic ups and downs, Central Canada's industries are usually shored up by subsidies—particularly in Quebec.

For decades, Bombardier and SNC Lavalin have been taking Canadians for billions of dollars. They have no incentive to practice better business principles and ethics. Their speciality is lobbying federal politicians. No party has the courage to say no to these corporations—they fear the electoral backlash from Quebec if there are layoffs. Western industries will always be milked to subsidize central Canadian manufacturing while federal politicians buy the region's electorate.

The preferential treatment of Central Canada's businesses isn't always as visible as it is with subsidies or government contracts. Sometimes it's regulatory, but it's no less odious.

While Air Canada was technically privatized back in 1989, it's been bailed out and subsidized so many times, it might as well still be a state-owned carrier.

Air Canada's decades with a near-monopoly on domestic air travel led to atrocious customer service and some of the most expensive airfares on the planet. WestJet began as an upstart regional airline out of Calgary offering air travel with a focus on customer service and low prices. The expansion of the airline was fast as Canadians—tired of Air Canada abuses—eagerly embraced the new provider. Air Canada begged the federal government to intervene in the market on their behalf and the government duly obliged! They couldn't let a Western Canadian business eat into the profits of their central Canadian business.

When WestJet tried to provide service to Toronto in 2004, Air Canada took the Greater Toronto Airport Authority to court to block the move and Justice James Farley of the Ontario Superior Court ruled in their favour. Toronto's Pearson International Airport had just expanded and added fourteen new gates for carriers. WestJet was supposed to have access to some of them, but the court ruling forced the airport to give them all to Air Canada. Air Canada was near insolvency at the time and didn't need the gates. They just sat on them to keep their competitors out. It was an outrageous court ruling, and it demonstrated the lengths to which the central Canadian establishment could and would go to prevent western industries from expanding into what they considered their turf.

Even the national employment insurance (EI) program is abused for federal electoral gain. To qualify for EI, a worker has to have been employed for a number of weeks. That threshold differs throughout regions, however. In the Maritimes, the bar is set much lower than in western regions.

Many high-calibre, hardworking employees have travelled west to make their fortune. Unfortunately, many others will only come long enough—a matter of weeks—to qualify for EI and then fly back east to collect those benefits for the rest of the season. In a healthy Confederation, people would be encouraged to relocate to prosperous regions rather than exploiting them to subsidize other regions that are absent of self-sustaining resources. Using programs like EI to buy Maritime votes is effective for electoral advantage, but it contributes to a national imbalance of labour pools and wealth. If you think a federal politician is coming to address the problem, don't hold your breath.

Examples of systemic regional bias are endless. In making the case for western independence, it's imperative we're ready to share examples of that bias. We must understand just how unfavourably the deck is stacked against the West within Confederation.

Chapter 3

A HISTORY OF ALIENATION

It's essential anyone who makes the case for western independence has a solid grounding in Canadian history in general and how the West specifically has been treated within Confederation. I won't go into the West's entire history, but I will set out some examples of how poorly it's been treated within Confederation.

It's striking how little has changed over the decades when it comes to Western alienation.

In a 1976 poll conducted by Dr. Roger Gibbins with the University of Calgary, researchers visited the homes of hundreds of Albertans to ask them their opinions on the issue. Those precise statements could be put to respondents again today and the answers would be much the same. The poll's statements with responses were as follows:

1. The economic policies of the federal government seem to help Quebec and Ontario at the expense of Alberta: 73.7 percent agreed, 9.6 percent disagreed.

2. Because the political parties depend on Quebec and Ontario for most of their votes, Alberta usually gets ignored in federal politics: 77.1 percent agreed, 13.9 percent disagreed.
3. During the past few years, the federal government has made a genuine effort to overcome the problems of economic discrimination against Alberta: 32.1 percent agreed, 45 percent disagreed.
4. In many ways, Alberta has more in common with the western United States than it does with Eastern Canada: 62.5 percent agreed, 18.9 percent disagreed.
5. Most eastern Canadians seem to feel that Canada ends at the Great Lakes: 64.5 percent agreed, 16.3 percent disagreed.
6. Alberta benefits as much from the industries of the East as Eastern Canada benefits from Alberta's natural resources such as oil: 23.9 percent agreed, 62.7 percent disagreed.
7. It often seems Alberta politicians are not taken seriously in the East: 71.3 percent agreed, 13.5 percent disagreed.
8. If one part of Canada suffers, we all suffer and if one region prospers, we all share in the prosperity: 32.1 percent agreed, 56.8 percent disagreed.
9. Albertans have to unite behind one party to get anything out of Ottawa: 63.9 percent agreed, 18.3 percent disagreed.

The issues and western attitudes towards them have remained unchanged for almost half a century since the poll was conducted.

It's clear feelings of alienation were strong years prior, even before the National Energy Program increased this sense of alienation and renewed eagerness for secessionism, pushing it to new levels.

Albertans were very aware they were getting a bad deal out of Confederation and they knew why.

Nearly 80 percent of those polled agreed that parties depend primarily on voter support from Ontario and Quebec and because of that will brush aside Alberta's needs. It isn't personal, though many take it personally—it's nothing more than political strategy. It also highlights how the system is broken as far as the West is concerned.

Most Central Canadians think little about anything West of the Ontario border, especially from a political perspective. Central Canadians don't generally hold westerners in contempt, they're just indifferent to us. This indifference is almost more infuriating than if they were simply to express contempt. While we've invested decades of hard work and contributed far more to Confederation than we've ever received in return, it seems we don't even register on the political radar of central Canadians, much less warrant any appreciation.

Pioneers and partisans

Beginning at Confederation, one can see how and why the foundations of regional inequity were established.

In the late 1800s, Western Canada was developing a thriving agrarian economy. The Prairies marked the new frontier and, by virtue of the Dominion Lands Act, millions of immigrants were drawn to the West in the hope of a new life as farmers. A quarter section of prairie land was handed over by the Dominion government to applicants for a $10 registration fee. There were strict conditions on its cultivation and ownership.

Laws in place to protect the interests of Central Canada put new homesteaders at an immediate disadvantage. Settlers were essentially forced into what amounted to indentured servitude—they were to hew wood and draw water, principally to serve central Canadian interests.

Much of the land within twenty miles of any rail line was initially reserved for the railway company itself. People could settle that land, but it first had to be purchased from the Canadian Pacific Railway company (CPR). This was one of many schemes created to help finance the construction of the railway across Canada. Central Canadian financiers wanted a return on their investment, which meant selling lands at a premium.

The exclusion zone around rail lines put cash-strapped western settlers at a huge disadvantage. Hauling farm implements and supplies to homesteads and transporting harvests to market was terribly difficult where farms were twenty or more miles from the nearest rail link. Towns were established close to rail links while many homesteaders were distanced on isolated farm plots. Land speculators with advance knowledge of rail routes of course prospered. The system was rife with corruption and insider trading. The demands on the meagre funds of settlers working to get established as farmers in the West represented the earliest transfer of wealth from westerners into the coffers of Central Canadians.

The exclusion zone around rail lines was eliminated in 1882, but the damage was done. Early settlers began their new lives with a sense of alienation and mistrust of central Canadian governance.

The constraints didn't end there. Most pioneers headed West with little more than a wagonload of supplies. They needed sturdier farm implements and tools to develop homesteads. While importing those goods from the United States would have been cheaper, federal government-imposed tariffs meant they were forced to buy goods manufactured in Central Canada. To add insult to injury, farmers had to pay freight fees to ship their implements over from Central Canada. They were then forced to pay them again for grain sent out at harvest time. They were getting squeezed from every which way and there was nothing they could do about it.

To be fair, the federal government did create the Crow Rate subsidy program to ease some of the shipping costs for western farmers. The program was controversial and a bone of contention for many politicians until the 1990s when then prime minister Jean Chrétien abolished it. In a more balanced and fair Confederation framework, such a subsidy would never have been necessary.

In 1904, the Canadian government granted provincial status to the western regions that encompassed the Prairies—formerly called the Northwest Territories. This of course turned into a political battle of Liberals versus Conservatives.

Fredrick Haultain was then premier of the Northwest Territories and was also a Conservative. He lobbied that the region should be one great prairie province with the name Buffalo. He believed the new province had to be geographically large enough so its inhabitants could stand up for themselves within Confederation.

Unfortunately, the Liberals won the 1904 election and the prime minister at the time Wilfred Laurier was in opposition to such a powerful entity being formed in the West. While its population was still sparse, its agricultural resources gave the region economic clout. Laurier split the territory into what is now Saskatchewan and Alberta and then gerrymandered the provincial seat distribution to ensure the first provincial governments would be Liberal. It took years to get them out, but once the Liberal governments were ejected from Saskatchewan and Alberta, they never returned to power again. The insecurity and jealous control exhibited by the Laurentian Elite in Central Canada has a long history.

Stakeholders and saboteurs

No history of western alienation is complete without some detail on the National Energy Program (NEP). The NEP was a four-year-long gross assault on Western Canada's economy beginning in 1980. A province's authority over its own natural resources was disregarded and a flourishing energy sector was crushed. Any lingering illusions that western provinces were equal within Confederation were shattered. It was made patently clear western provinces were little more than regional colonies to be milked of their resources by the federal government. We were then and remain still a subservient region within Canada allowed to exercise regional autonomy only when it's considered by Ottawa convenient to do so.

It's been over forty years since the NEP. Anyone who lived in the West at the time would remember it well. Liberal support in the West among people aged over sixty is still almost non-existent to this day and the NEP is much of the reason why. Younger generations have never experienced this kind of assault on a region's industrial sectors. They should be educated about what unfolded and understand that it could happen again.

Indeed, as inflation soars again in Canada and oil prices rise, yet another Trudeau sits at the nation's helm. It appears we are seeing history repeat itself. We must never forget what the West has endured. The story of the NEP must be told and retold so it will be remembered.

The historical background of that odious policy is important to understand. It's eerily similar to what's happening today. It's amazing how little has really changed.

Western Canada's petrochemical industry was one of the later entries into the ranks of the world energy powers. While natural gas was discovered in Medicine Hat in 1905 and oil in Turner Valley in 1914, it wasn't until the 1950s that the West became a major petrochemical manufacturer.

In 1947, Alberta was providing only 10 percent of Canada's total oil requirement. Most of Canada's oil needs were being met by Venezuela and the US. Albertan oil was considered expensive and inconvenient. Western producers and politicians lobbied for policies to encourage Canadian consumption of Albertan products, but the pro-West lobbyists were usually turned away. Oil refining was big business in Central Canada and Laurentian-owned companies had built a successful energy empire using imported oil products, so they fought to preserve their position.

To be fair, the policy of refusing to impose tariffs on foreign oil was a helpful one. Protectionism rarely serves consumers and typically causes an imbalance in the development and growth of industries. Canada's hands-off approach to western oil and gas producers would change dramatically, however, when commodity prices exploded in the 1970s.

With eastern Canadian investors showing no interest in participating in western energy development and the federal government indifferent to the fate of western industries, producers unsurprisingly sought investment and markets elsewhere. American investors were keen for a stake in Alberta's oil development. Before long, most of the oil and gas companies in the province were connected to American interests.

With the discovery of the rich Leduc oilfield in 1947, Alberta's oil and gas industry truly began to take off. The Trans Mountain Pipeline was constructed to transport oil to BC and Washington State while another pipeline network carried oil to the United States and Sarnia, Ontario. Americans remained the most enthusiastic investors and customers for the West's oil and gas products while fields were developed.

In the early 1960s, Western oil producers formed the Independent Petroleum Association of Canada industry lobby (IPAC). IPAC pitched to the Government of Canada that an extension of the oil pipeline that terminated in Sarnia should be extended to Montreal to supply 150,000 to 200,000 barrels of oil per day by 1970.

IPAC's brief said: "Canada is the only nation capable of self-sufficiency [and] gives only limited priority to domestic oil, permits a drain of hundreds of millions of dollars for overseas oil, leaves half the nation totally dependent on overseas supplies, thus ignoring the problem of security in emergencies, and leaves it to another nation—the United States—to provide the lion's share of market growth for a Canadian resource."

The federal government rejected the proposals. They told IPAC that Venezuela had to be protected as a source and that western Canadian oil was simply too expensive. The West was told to focus its efforts on selling oil and gas to the American Midwest. Ottawa told the West that they didn't want our oil and that we should sell it elsewhere, so we did.

Ottawa's tune was to change dramatically when the OPEC-induced oil crisis hit in the early 1970s. Suddenly, Pierre Trudeau's Liberal government decided Alberta's "expensive" oil was to become

Canada's oil and was to be sold to the East at a discount. This was how the NEP was born.

In 1973, OPEC cut oil production and imposed an export embargo against the United States and other countries that had supported Israel during the Yom Kippur War. OPEC was a cartel of oil-producing nations dominated by Arab states, but also included Venezuela. OPEC's actions led to price shocks causing world crude oil prices to quadruple.

While the OPEC embargo was only in place for a little over six months, its impact remained for more than a decade. North America was driven into recession while high energy prices caused rampant inflation. American President Richard Nixon and Prime Minister Pierre Trudeau responded with wage and price controls that were catastrophic and served only to exacerbate economic woes.

When the OPEC embargo was over, oil prices remained high. With wage and price controls a proven failure, Trudeau took another page out of the socialist's handbook and initiated steps towards the nationalization of oil and gas production with the creation of Petro-Canada. Rather than admit the failure of his government's domestic policies, Trudeau blamed western energy companies accusing them of price gouging. He was convinced a state-owned oil company would balance the market.

Petro-Canada was created by the Trudeau government in 1975 with an injection of 1.5 billion in Canadian tax dollars. It was to be a Canada-owned oil and gas company proposing to offset the dominance of American ownership in western Canadian energy companies. The West's oil Central Canada had previously found so undesirable was now so precious that the government was moved to form its own energy company in order to exploit it.

Central Canada's indifference to energy resource development in Western Canada had previously driven the sector into partnership with the US. Now, the collaboration was considered so problematic that nationalization of the resources was deemed the only solution.

Petro-Canada was not well received by Albertan producers. After decades of being spurned by Central Canada, producers now had to compete with an oil and gas producer that was backstopped with millions of tax dollars. Large red office buildings were constructed in Calgary to house Petro-Canada's operations. Rather than celebrate these new edifices, Albertans derisively dubbed the towers "Red Square" to mock the socialist spirit of their creation.

Petro-Canada hired thousands of people and those who worked for the company had to be discreet about their jobs—being in the employ of Pierre Trudeau was hardly a badge of honour in Alberta. When the gas stations first opened in Alberta, few would dare to be seen patronizing them. Indeed, Petro-Canada was so loathed in the region, it had to disguise its gas stations under different names to avoid an outright boycott. You might recall those odd penguin- and dinosaur-themed gas stations that were around Calgary until the 1990s. They were actually camouflaged Petro-Canada stations.

As is typical with state-owned companies, Petro-Canada managed to consistently operate at a loss until it was eventually privatized in 1991. Petro-Canada's attempted takeover of Husky Energy in the 1970s was also a fiasco and remains to this day a case study in horribly incompetent business management. Husky Energy is now amalgamated with Cenovus.

While Petro-Canada was an imposing force in the industry with its huge tax subsidies, it was still a laughingstock within the sector. Their business strategies proved terrible. In a highly competitive environment, private companies constantly outmanoeuvred Petro-Canada.

When it became clear a state-owned oil and gas entity was not going to take western Canada's energy sector by storm, Trudeau used legislation as a stick—or rather a hammer—to beat western energy companies into submission. He introduced the NEP in 1980.

The NEP was the largest regional wealth grab in Canadian history. Its stated intention was to secure domestic energy supplies and eliminate dependence on the world oil market while ensuring Alberta's oil profits were shared throughout the country. Rather than respond with contrition over the results of their poor domestic energy policies,

Ottawa came with the hammer. Albertans were painted as greedy "blue-eyed sheiks" profiting at the expense of all Canadians. The Trudeau government manipulated Canadians by leveraging the politics of regional envy and division and swooped in on the West's profitable and burgeoning energy sector.

Ottawa imposed an 8-percent tax on oil development while forcing producers to sell oil within Canada at a significant discount. Tariffs were imposed on oil exports and taxes were introduced on natural gas and liquid gas sales. The federal take on oil and gas revenues increased 140 percent and a "backing-in" provision forced oil and gas companies to turn over 25 percent of their properties to the federal government. Even Stalin would have blushed at such a move.

The effect was immediate. Energy companies laid off employees, shuttered their doors, and left the country. Alberta's economy was decimated. Mortgage interest rates hovered between 15 and 20 percent as the Bank of Canada tried to battle rampant inflation. Many newly unemployed Albertans had to walk away from their mortgages. The term "jingle mail" was coined at the time for Albertan's who would mail their keys to the bank and vacating their homes.

Rather than increase domestic energy security, the NEP had the opposite effect. The number of drilling projects for new oil and gas wells diminished to a fraction of what it had been. Production levels soon dropped in a similar fashion. Hundreds of drilling rigs moved south of the border along with thousands of professionals from the industry. While the federal government continued to soak Petro-Canada with tax subsidies, it couldn't come close to filling the void created by the NEP.

The vacuous myth persisted awhile that oil companies in Canada would stick around no matter how awful the abuses. The NEP put lie to that myth, but it would appear still the lesson was wasted.

When Ed Stelmach was Alberta's premier, he considered gouging the industry with a royalty hike and consequently drove investment from the province. Companies are fleeing Western Canada even today as Prime Minister Justin Trudeau muses about shutting down the West's entire oil and gas sector.

The presence of abundant natural resources is hardly a guarantee of prosperity. If it were so, Venezuela would be one of the richest nations on earth. Instead, in 2017 while surrounded by oil reserves, people in Venezuela were reported to have been eating zoo animals to survive.

It's estimated the NEP drained Alberta of up to $100 billion. In 1980s terms, those funds would have gone a very long way towards diversifying the West's economy. Or perhaps those energy revenues could have been saved in a pension fund just as Norway did and by doing so created the world's largest sovereign wealth fund.

Conservative leader Brian Mulroney campaigned against the NEP in the 1984 federal election. Western voters widely supported him particularly for his stand challenging the NEP. Mulroney went on to win the election by a landslide becoming Canada's 18th prime minister. However, he refused to dismantle the NEP for another two and a half years.

By then, oil prices had dropped so low Canada would've had to pay a higher price for oil in order to subsidize Alberta. While the NEP capped the price Alberta could sell oil to the rest of the country for, it also had a minimum price the rest of the country was supposed to pay if world oil prices dropped. This was the flip side of the NEP. The moment the NEP looked as though it might benefit Alberta, it was scrapped. Alberta was taken to the cleaners both when coming and going.

Oil prices in 1980 were US$37.42 per barrel. Prices remained high until 1986 when they fell to US$14.44 per barrel. The Mulroney Conservatives happily continued to drain Alberta until world oil prices dropped.

Some claim it was low oil prices that decimated Alberta's economy. As I explain, it's simply not true. World oil prices were well within a profitable range for Alberta throughout the entire duration of the NEP, yet Alberta's economy fell apart at the beginning of the program.

Mulroney's actions illustrated that it matters not which party is in government. Be it Liberal or Conservative, the government will serve the interests of Central Canada every time. Ending the NEP was a convenient campaign platform to win western votes, and it was only abolished once its purpose had been served and until it became incompatible with Central Canada's interests.

In 1988, I moved from Banff, Alberta, into an apartment in downtown Calgary. I clearly remember the multitude of half-constructed buildings with motionless cranes sitting forlornly and silently atop them. The NEP had hit Alberta's economy so hard and so rapidly that building construction was halted immediately. Slowly but surely the cranes began to haul and swing again, but it would be several years—well into the 1990s—before those half-finished buildings were complete.

Central Canada's utter indifference to the needs of the West during the NEP era must never be forgotten. The federal government neither consulted the West nor apologized for the damage they inflicted on the Western community. Our economic welfare was apparently a trifling matter as far as the federal government was concerned before, during, and after the NEP fiasco.

Don't think for a second the feds couldn't or wouldn't do it again. Only independence will protect us from such devastating incursions in the future.

Chapter 4

THE ALBERTA AGENDA AND OTHER INDEPENDENCE DEFERRAL EFFORTS

In 2000, many westerners were apprehensive when the federal Reform Party of Canada was dissolved to form the Canadian Alliance in the hopes of winning Central Canadian votes. Westerners had invested over a decade with the Reform Party with the message "the West wants in." Feelings of western alienation were cleverly exploited with the slogan. It implied not only that Western Canada wanted to be heard, but also that it wanted a role in national affairs. It appeared at the time we might be giving up all that hard-won ground and turning back into the same old Progressive Conservative Party, indistinguishable from the federal Liberal Party when it came to regional issues. It took two conventions and a lot of pressure from political tall-foreheads before party members were convinced reluctantly to accept a mountain of compromise and form a new party.

The Canadian Alliance was an electoral washout. The party failed to make a breakthrough in Eastern Canada during the 2000 election while Chrétien's Liberals increased their seat count.

Western Canadians were furious and dejected. We had been patient. We had compromised. We had endured an entire campaign, which appeared to have been designed to insult and marginalize us. We had come out of it with nothing. Our regional party was gone and we were facing four more years of federal governance under a prime minister who held our region in open contempt. Support for western independence suddenly skyrocketed to heights unseen since the despised National Energy Program was imposed on the West by Pierre Trudeau in the 1980s.

The Canadian Alliance was dissolved. It merged with the remnants of the Progressive Conservative Party and rebranded as the Conservative Party of Canada (CPC). Stephen Harper was elected leader of the new entity and independence movements cooled. With one of the signatories of the Alberta Agenda serving as prime minister, the West would surely get a fair shake in Confederation, right?

While Harper eventually managed to win a majority government with the CPC, he only served a single term with a majority and no significant change was made to Canada's system. We have of course languished under Liberal governments ever since. The default government in Canada is Liberal because Central Canada is Liberal. That won't change.

The Alberta Agenda

Shortly after its founding, the Alberta Independence Party failed. It was the result of poor organization and my own inept leadership. Another contributory factor that hindered the party's establishment was the creation of the Alberta Agenda.

At the end of January 2001, the release of the Alberta Agenda letter promptly took a lot of wind from our sails. Support for independence can be soft and people will typically reach out for alternatives rather than navigate secession's challenging course. The Alberta Agenda gave people new hope. They abandoned independence efforts in 2001 just as they had at the end of the 1980s when the Reform Party hit the scene.

The Alberta Agenda was an open letter penned and signed by Stephen Harper, Ted Morton, Tom Flanagan, Rainer Knopff, Andrew Crooks, and Ken Boessenkool. It was addressed to then premier Ralph Klein and was published in the *National Post*. The letter listed five things that could be done within the province of Alberta to create a firewall against incursions from an increasingly hostile federal government.

The tenets of the Alberta Agenda are below, quoted directly:

- Withdraw from the Canada Pension Plan to create an Alberta Pension Plan offering the same benefits at lower cost while giving Alberta control over the investment fund. Pensions are a provincial responsibility under section 94A of the Constitution

Act, 1867; and the legislation setting up the Canada Pension Plan permits a province to run its own plan, as Quebec has done from the beginning. If Quebec can do it, why not Alberta?

- Collect our own revenue from personal income tax, as we already do for corporate income tax. Now that your government has made the historic innovation of the single-rate personal income tax, there is no reason to have Ottawa collect our revenue. Any incremental cost of collecting our own personal income tax would be far outweighed by the policy flexibility that Alberta would gain, as Quebec's experience has shown.
- Start preparing now to let the contract with the RCMP run out in 2112 and create an Alberta Provincial Police Force. Alberta is a major province. Like the other major provinces of Ontario and Quebec, we should have our own provincial police force. We have no doubt that Alberta can run a more efficient and effective police force than Ottawa can—one that will not be misused as a laboratory for experiments in social engineering.
- Resume provincial responsibility for health-care policy. If Ottawa objects to provincial policy, fight in the courts. If we lose, we can afford the financial penalties that Ottawa may try to impose under the Canada Health Act. Albertans deserve better than the long waiting periods and technological backwardness that are rapidly coming to characterize Canadian medicine. Alberta should also argue that each province should raise its own revenue for health-care—i.e., replace Canada Health and Social Transfer cash with tax points, as Quebec has argued for many

years. Poorer provinces would continue to rely on Equalization to ensure they have adequate revenues.

- Use section 88 of the Supreme Court's decision in the Quebec Secession Reference to force Senate reform back onto the national agenda. Our reading of that decision is that the federal government and other provinces must seriously consider a proposal for constitutional reform endorsed by "a clear majority on a clear question" in a provincial referendum. You acted decisively once before to hold a senatorial election. Now is the time to drive the issue further.

While support for western independence in early 2001 was at an all-time high, it was still mostly driven by what I would call reluctant secessionists. Westerners were at the end of their rope and were beginning to accept that only independence would change the status quo, but many still wanted to find a way to give Confederation one last shot. They wanted a lifeline before they committed to cutting the cord on Confederation. The Alberta Agenda gave them a glimmer of hope they could still somehow fix Canada from within.

The letter offered a plan outlining how Albertans could distance themselves from Ottawa without a battle on the federal front or demanding independence. The changes proffered could all be achieved within existing provincial jurisdiction. Indeed, many of the policies proposed within the Alberta Agenda were already in place in some eastern provinces.

The Alberta Agenda's impact on the momentum of our nascent party was immediate and devastating. New membership sales declined and many existing members stepped back saying, "We don't need to go the independence route. We can implement the Alberta Agenda within the existing government."

Premier Ralph Klein never implemented a single aspect of the Alberta Agenda during his tenure, neither did Stephen Harper move to implement or facilitate any aspects of the Agenda while he was in power as prime minister. While former premier Jason Kenney paid lip service to the Alberta Agenda with his Fair Deal panels' hearings across the province, he didn't implement any aspects of the Alberta Agenda during his term either. Kenney's reluctance to stand up to Ottawa was a primary reason members of his own party revolted and pushed him from leadership. People are getting tired of broken promises on provincial autonomy and are starting to hold politicians accountable. This is a healthy development.

To date, the Alberta Agenda appears to have been nothing more than a carrot and stick used to quell regional discontent while never having actually achieved anything to address it. It doesn't mean the Alberta Agenda has no value. The need for the Agenda's propositions is as great now as it's ever been. We need to change our end goal and strategy.

Instead of viewing the Alberta Agenda and other similar initiatives as tools to stave off western independence movements, we should view them as steps *towards* independence.

The policy framework within the Alberta Agenda will not stop Ottawa from infringing provincial jurisdiction. Nothing within the Alberta Agenda will stem the fiscal bleed of the West by Central Canada. It will not help get our energy projects up and running in the face of Ottawa's opposition. What those policies *will* do, though, is inch us closer to the doorway of full independence. Looking at them through this lens, those policies and initiatives look much more appealing.

Policing the provinces

It's argued a provincial police force wouldn't offer more operational efficiency over the RCMP. While that's debatable, it really doesn't matter when the intent of the formation of the force is to disconnect westerners further from Ottawa. It would be one less question-mark issue to wrangle during an independence referendum.

Having a provincial police force prevents the federal government from diminishing our protections and security. And provinces have unique policing needs all their own. While in early 2022, RCMP officers from across Canada were sent into Ottawa to quell the Canadian Freedom Convoy protests, eco-terrorists chose that same moment to target a pipeline project in Northern BC. More than twenty axe-wielding extremists violently attacked security guards and workers while setting traps to block any police response. All the attackers escaped and no arrests were made. It could have ended quite differently had there been a large provincial police team available to respond, rather than a depleted RCMP force.

Every western province should form its own police force. Provinces can't change federal laws, but their local police forces can choose whether to enforce them. Let Ottawa send the RCMP in to enforce unjust laws on their own dime, if they are insistent.

The federal government is ideologically opposed to resource development in Western Canada. Although they're not supposedly supporting eco-terrorist attempts to shut down the West's projects, they don't seem terribly bothered by them, either. We need local police forces acting under the guidance of provincial governments to ensure our policing needs come first. That's worth far more than any potential monetary savings gained by maintaining the RCMP as our primary rural police force.

Don't forget, RCMP services are not gifted to us by Ottawa; we contract them and pay from our provincial budgets. Those funds can be redirected to a provincial force. Furthermore, it can be assumed many of the current RCMP members would leave the federal force and join a new provincial police service.

Evolution is long overdue in the police service. The movement to "defund the police" is primarily based on spite and identity politics, however, policing in Western Canada *does* need a systemic overhaul. Rather than trying to tweak and modify entrenched attitudes within the RCMP service, we would be better served by creating an entirely new force with a modern mandate and training process. The creation of provincial police forces in Western Canada would also help move us a little further from federal control.

Any new police service could and should have regulations and mandates to stymie the government's ability to politicize police investigations. Prime Minister Justin Trudeau has repeatedly and directly interfered in judicial process in Canada. Trudeau breached the Conflict of Interest Act when he meddled in the SNC Lavalin case in 2017 and when he visited the island of the Aga Khan—both scandals without satisfactory conclusion. Documents released in 2019 indicate RCMP investigators believed there were "reasonable grounds" to conclude the prime minister had committed fraud in the Aga Khan scandal, yet they chose not to press charges. Should this come as any surprise when the prime minister directly appoints the head of the RCMP?

It appears in the spring of 2020, RCMP Commissioner Brenda Lucki might have been interfering at the behest of the Prime Minister's Office in the investigation of the Nova Scotia mass shooting. It's infuriating to consider the Prime Minister's Office might have meddled in the investigation into the worst mass shooting in Canadian history while the bodies were still warm, yet evidence indicates it happened. Evidence and experience also tell us the prime minister won't face sanctions or charges over this criminal breach of trust. If the nation's police force can be influenced so blatantly—and without consequences—it cannot be trusted.

Political leaders shouldn't be charged on a whim, but neither should they ever be above the law of the land. It's an affront to democracy that the prime minister has sole authority over the selection of the chief of the RCMP. Under such circumstances, the RCMP will never be a force independent from the federal government. Provincial forces, on the other hand, could have their political independence legislated. Control of the force should never be put into the hands of a single individual.

Where the taxman lives

Separating provincial and federal levels of personal income tax filing is a redundant exercise and it only serves to swell bureaucracy in the system. However, when the goal is a freestanding tax collection system that would assume all income tax collection in a post-independence West, it makes sense to set up that infrastructure sooner rather than later.

Quebec collects its provincial taxes separately from the federal tax. Some are under the misunderstanding that Quebec collects all taxes and remits the federal portion to Ottawa; it isn't the case, and neither would it be the case if Alberta implemented a similar policy. The policy just separates the two forms and the collection. Provinces already collect corporate taxes this way.

We need to sever every possible connection with the federal government before we get to an independence referendum, and taxation collection an important one. It's one less item we would need to address during the campaign and one less to deal with afterwards.

Pension fair play

The age demographic in Canada means Albertans have consistently paid much more into the Canada Pension Plan (CPP) than they've received. It is, of course, consistent with many programs within Confederation. In establishing and entrenching a provincial pension plan ahead of independence, western provinces could offer security to seniors and to those approaching retirement in the knowledge they'll still be supported. It would be another task complete before a vote to secede.

Many senior westerners have fears about being left without a pension if the West were to become independent. There'd be no better way to reassure seniors that the fruits of their lifetime of labour are secure than to have an independent, fully funded provincial pension plan already in place. Quebec has long had its own pension plan and it has served their retired population well. There's no reason why western provinces can't do the same. Why not set it up now?

Seniors are often the strongest supporters of western independence. They've had to endure not only one but two Trudeau prime ministers. They're also the population demographic most likely to get out and vote in elections and referendums. Their concerns need to be taken seriously. Fears over losing their pension return on investment are legitimate. Provincial pension plans would ensure retirement security, but the concept needs to be sold to concerned citizens. If the federal government acts in bad faith in transferring CPP balances to seniors in western provinces, the provinces need to ensure seniors know they won't be left out to dry. Maintaining people's dependence on the federal government for retirement funding has been an effective way to stifle growth in support of independence. We need to address this dependence.

The health of a nation

In every provincial election, health care is always the prevailing issue among voters. The Canadian establishment has for decades perpetuated the myth that Canada has the best health care system in the world. That edifice is beginning to crumble as citizens languish on interminable waiting lists for medical procedures, while others with means leave the country to seek care in countries where they can buy it. The need for health care reform is acute, but it won't happen under Canada's rigid and inefficient Health Act.

Provinces should start reforming their health care systems and base them on successful European models despite the federal Health Act.

Unless Ottawa suddenly starts paying 50 percent of our provincial health care costs—as was stipulated by the original Medical Care Act—why the hell should we let them dictate how we run our system? As far as the courts are concerned, the cards are stacked against us and we would surely lose any challenge, but those battles would serve to *entrench* support for independence. We would make progress by building an independent health care system that will serve us come independence. Let's get the ball rolling.

Red-herring politics

Since the Alberta Agenda, there have been several other high-profile initiatives purporting to support western autonomy.

The Buffalo Declaration was released on February 20, 2020. It was a manifesto created by four Albertan federal MPs. It was a response to the growing secessionist movement that sprouted in response to the 2019 re-election of the Trudeau government.

The Buffalo Declaration contained all sorts of tough talk. It laid out the historical grievances of the West at length.

It stated, "Alberta is treated as a colony, rather than an equal partner in Confederation."

It boldly declared, "We will not continue to be milked for equalization payments while our right to work is stolen from us."

The declaration laid out a number of demands from Ottawa from constitutional reform to mandating regional balance in programs for infrastructure funding. Then, poof! The Buffalo Declaration disappeared.

The website is still there. The MPs who wrote the document remained MPs. What about the declaration? We never heard another peep about it.

Every MP who signed the declaration toed the party line and was deathly silent about it during the 2021 election. They lined up like good little partisans and remained silent as CPC leader Erin O'Toole screwed the West with his carbon tax flip-flop and ran a losing federal election campaign almost exclusively out of Ontario.

The Buffalo Declaration had served its purpose. It calmed the ruffled feathers of westerners—to a degree—so the federal Conservative party could then position itself to win the hearts of Central Canada's voters. It gave westerners false hope that federal members of government might stand up for them. I have some bad news, kiddos; even if O'Toole had won, our issues wouldn't have made it onto the federal agenda. How many times do we have to go down this road?

The Buffalo Declaration was a strategic tool used to marginalize independence supporters. It was effective. We need to be cognizant of this kind of independence deferral effort and stop falling for it.

The Free Alberta Strategy initiatives were released shortly after the 2021 election and were created by lawyers Derek From and Rob Anderson, and also professor of political science, Dr. Barry Cooper.

The Free Alberta Strategy is much like the Alberta Agenda, but it does have a more militant feel about it. It speaks of making Alberta a "sovereign jurisdiction within Canada." The strategy calls for provocative measures on the part of the provincial government that include many unilateral actions. It advocates for opting out of EI and CPP and taking control of foreign trade.

The strategy, if pursued by the province, will undoubtedly invoke a constitutional crisis. The authors of the document make no bones about that. They know the Ottawa establishment will push back and that the courts will strike down the measures taken by Alberta.

The strategy then calls for provincial independence as a final resort. It lays out some of the steps required to put the control of the independence process into the hands of Albertans.

Rob Anderson is a top advisor for Alberta Premier Danielle Smith. Smith's proposed Sovereignty Act Within a United Canada is based on the Free Alberta Strategy. Smith is taking the strongest stance on provincial autonomy ever adopted by a western premier. The battle lines are being drawn and eventually provincial autonomy efforts will end up before the federally appointed Supreme Court. There, the efforts will fail. That's not to say efforts were pointless; they are all steps in the creation of the foundation for full independence. Provinces need to take the fight to Ottawa and lose repeatedly. *This* is how citizens will come to realize and accept that the system is fundamentally broken. And when they do, they'll be ready to pursue a path to full independence.

Slowly but painfully, we are working towards western independence. The Alberta Agenda lays out steps we can take. While the authors of the Buffalo Declaration proved to be politically toothless, they made some good points in their document. Every step in the Free Alberta Strategy is also worth pursuing since they all move us closer to independence. However, we must be careful not to see these statements, strategies, and policy papers as alternatives to full independence—they are merely steps towards it.

Examine these efforts, but do not be tempted by the notion that the system can be repaired. Every time an initiative on provincial autonomy fails, it causes the number of people dedicated to full western independence to grow.

We can't sit back with an independence-or-nothing attitude. We will surely end up with nothing. We need to continue supporting genuine efforts to distance western provinces from Ottawa's control while never forgetting that full independence remains the singular long-term goal.

Chapter 5

THE REFERENDUM

The only way to achieve independence will be via referendum where a majority of citizens choose independence on a clear question. This is a requirement from a legislative and moral viewpoint. There are no shortcuts and we can't waste any time pursuing them.

In October 1995, Quebec citizens went to the polls to answer this referendum question: "Do you agree that Quebec should become sovereign after having made a formal offer to Canada for a new economic and political partnership within the scope of the bill respecting the future of Quebec and of the agreement signed on June 12, 1995?"

The question on the ballot was quite a mouthful. It was purposely crafted to be ambiguous to secure a yes vote. Quebec's independence proponents used the question to play both sides of the fence. Some said it was a vote on independence, others said it was a statement made to ensure stronger provincial rights. Despite the confusing question, most agreed the referendum was about independence.

An astounding 93.52 percent of the Quebec population turned out to vote. The yes side lost by a very slim margin—just over 1 percent. Controversy was assured with such a close result.

On referendum night, then Quebec premier Jacques Parizeau said that "money and ethnic votes" was the reason the yes side lost. It was clear he was blaming the loss on the considerable Jewish population of Montreal. Parizeau resigned as premier and leader of the Parti Québécois the next day.

With the yes side having come so close to victory, federalists were quite rattled. They blamed the convoluted ballot question and claimed it caused voter confusion. It's hard to argue with the federalists on this point. The federal government responded the absence of clear language in Quebec's referendum by creating the 1999 Clarity Act.

The Clarity Act gave the House of Commons the power to ensure a proposed referendum question was considered unambiguous before going to a public vote. The act was specific in that it stated any referendum question would be invalid if it did not clearly state its goal was secession. This ruled out word trickery and deception by proponents of independence on referendum questions. This is good legislation. If a province can't get a majority vote for independence without having to resort to questionable phrasing of the ballot question in a referendum, the province simply isn't ready to secede.

The creators of the Clarity Act hoped that by requiring clear language in any referendum on independence, they would strengthen Canadian unity. The Federalists who created the act truly believed no province would ever have a majority seek independence. They believed a clear question in a referendum would always get a no vote. Federalists were in denial that so many Quebec citizens wanted out of Confederation. However, when the votes came, independence advocates had come within 1 percent of victory. It was easier to blame the question's phrasing than admit millions of Quebecers wanted to leave Canada.

Despite the Clarity Act, not only did legislators fail to quell nationalistic regionalism in Canada, they also created a roadmap to independence for all Canadian provinces and territories. The federal government legitimized the right and the ability to pursue and achieve full independence via referendum. The Clarity Act doesn't just call for clear and concise referendum questions, it also obligates Canada to negotiate in good faith with any province that—with a clear ballot question—has voted to secede. I'm not inclined to support federalist efforts from Ottawa, but I am delighted with the requirements of the Clarity Act.

I wouldn't be in support of the secession of any province unless I was convinced a majority had clearly demanded it. A binding referendum with a clearly worded question on the ballot is the only way to confidently establish majority will is represented. Success will come when we've rallied a meaningful majority of the population to vote to leave the Confederation in a proper referendum. From a legal and moral standpoint, nothing else will do. How, in good conscience, can we demand Confederation be dismantled if a referendum is not executed in good faith?

Over the years I've heard countless theories pushed about how the West can bypass democratic means and secede from Confederation. Some claim we're all sovereign individuals and we need simply to declare ourselves independent. Some claim provinces were never part of Confederation to begin with. Some felt the late Queen Elizabeth II could declare us independent. All these theories are pure bunk. Not only does the discussion sidetrack any real progress towards western independence, but they also make us look crazy. These theories and discussions will always pop up, but no serious movement should entertain or promote them. There are no substitutes for a democratic and fair referendum.

Beyond the obvious need for majority public support, it will take several steps before any western province arrives at a point where a successful referendum on independence can be held.

While Quebec had multiple referendums on independence initiated by their provincial governments, westerners can't assume their provincial governments will offer referendums to the citizens. We need to put the power to initiate referendums directly into the hands of citizens.

Westerners need to lobby for and establish legislation that provides for binding, citizen-initiated referenda legislation. Governments often campaign on and pay lip service to direct democracy initiatives, but they rarely follow through and empower citizens to do so. Politicians jealously guard their monopoly on legislation. It will take heavy pressure and persistent lobbying to force any government to craft effective, citizen-driven referenda legislation.

In the 2019 Alberta election, Jason Kenney's UCP election platform included measures for direct democracy. After achieving majority government, however, the UCP quickly reneged on their direct democracy promises. Pressure from party members and plummeting poll results forced the UCP begrudgingly to relent in the spring of 2021 and give Alberta a form of citizens' initiative legislation. Unfortunately, the UCP government slipped measures into the legislation that rendered it virtually useless. It was a crass bait-and-switch tactic to get grassroots members off their case while not empowering citizens at all.

If people in Alberta want to initiate a referendum on any aspect of constitutional change, they need 20 percent of registered voters in the province to sign an official petition. Proponents have a 90-day period within which to get these signatures. Those requirements make it virtually impossible for anyone to initiate a referendum outside of government.

It would take over 550,000 signatures inside three months to initiate a referendum. This is unlike an internet petition. Official petitions require a physical signature along with an address and phone number. It must also be witnessed. Many people concerned with privacy simply will not sign. Neither is it easy to catch people at home and convince them to sign a petition. On average, the electoral office rejects 10 percent of signatures on petitions because signees are not on the voter list, addresses are incorrect, handwriting is illegible, and other such reasons. Almost 7,000 signatures per day would need to be gathered for 90 consecutive days to trigger a referendum. An outstanding petitioner might perhaps gather 100 signatures per day. It would take nearly one hundred full-time petitioners working five days per week for three months straight to get the required signatures. Let's be clear, it simply won't happen and the government knows it. Their legislation was an insult to proponents of direct democracy.

With a referendum essential to independence, it becomes critically important for proponents to acquire the means to trigger a referendum. Governments must be heavily pressured to provide realistic referendum legislation. Among the many things on the to-do checklist for independence activists, this is a big one.

When favourable conditions for a successful independence referendum are achieved and assuming a province has reasonable citizens' initiative legislation already in place, one of the toughest challenges for independence activists will then present itself. All pro-independence organizations will need to *unite* in one mission to get independence on a ballot for citizens. No referendum will come if there are half a dozen scattered petition campaign initiatives from different groups. Even assuming a reasonable bar has been set, there's no doubt tens of thousands of signatures will be needed. Activist groups must set aside personal grudges and competitive differences in order to work together on a single petition in pursuit of an independence referendum. It will also mean fewer squabbles if the ballot carries a clear unambiguous yes-or-no question.

Once a referendum date is set and the campaign begins, groups can move back into their camps and work however it suits them to promote a yes vote. It will be integral to a campaign's progress that one group is delegated to dominate ground-level organization of the referendum campaign—choosing which group is potentially challenging for obvious reasons. The referendum campaign will be much like an electoral campaign—good central organization being paramount.

As with any campaign, voter identification and efficient get-out-the-vote (GOTV) campaigns will be crucial to a yes-vote victory. Volunteers will need to be gathered and trained to campaign. Door knocking, phone campaigning, and literature drops must ensue. If multiple groups don't coordinate, many voters will find themselves contacted several times each, while others might get overlooked for the entire campaign. On voting day, supporters could end up barraged by calls from multiple GOTV groups while other supporters languish without a reminder to cast a ballot.

Although by itself, support for independence could indeed be strong enough to win a yes vote in a referendum campaign, complacence would be foolhardy. We would have to keep noses to the grindstone for the best possible victory margin. We will need campaigns to be as effective and efficient as possible and it will require solid central leadership. The plan for that leadership role should be laid out well before a campaign is triggered to avoid time wasted infighting and jockeying.

We must persevere and keep our eye on the only prize that matters—independence. Each and every step of a referendum campaign will be critical. We will need to work together, no matter what.

Advocates for independence should be well versed in the referendum process and maintain a consistent plan. The plan begins with the initiation of the referendum and following through to a meaningful victory. While a referendum win might technically be a vote of 50 percent plus one, for the sake of peace and a smooth transition, we should set the bar much higher. It will require a strong and well-orchestrated plan for a referendum. It would be a grand pity if a referendum were lost to a poorly executed campaign rather than a true lack of public support for independence. Now is the time to start thinking about that campaign. We cannot begin planning too early.

Chapter 6

PATIENCE IS INDEED A VIRTUE

I know. I get it. You've concluded the system is broken and want out of it, yesterday. You want a referendum and to get to work on the process of creating an independent West. I don't blame you and I share your frustration. We must temper our impatience, though, and as tough as that might be, we simply aren't ready to go, yet.

If I could go back in time and talk to my twenty-nine-year-old self, patience is the first lesson I would share. This is a long game. We have to stop making mistakes in our zeal to break free from a broken system.

People are constantly demanding an immediate referendum on secession and I can't this stress strongly enough: it's the worst thing we could possibly do, right now.

Divide and conquer

Quebec has many true and dedicated secessionists. Their provincial government is full of them, so is the Bloc Québécois. They could call a referendum at any time. So, why haven't they?

Some people think Quebec simply likes to threaten to leave, but in truth doesn't really want to and that Quebec prefers to perpetually threaten secession as a way to get concessions from the rest of Canada. And, yes, some pragmatic politicians within Quebec are doing just that. But let's not fool ourselves, there's a strong base of support for independence in Quebec and they want out no matter how harsh the economic consequences of independence might be for their province.

The reason Quebec hasn't held an independence referendum since 1995 is they know they would lose. If support for independence in the province ever exceeds a measurable 60 percent, rest assured there would be a new referendum. They're biding their time.

The main basis of Quebec's independence movement is linguistic and cultural. Quebec's government is dominated by independence supporters, but rather than advocating for secession, they are trying their hardest to create the winning conditions for a referendum by slowly manipulating the demographics of their population. They have used increasingly oppressive legislation against non-French speakers in the hope of driving them from the province. They don't care about losing citizens, even if it costs them their economic strength. They simply want to ensure French speakers dominate the population enough so a referendum on secession would result in their favour.

After the 1995 Quebec independence referendum ended in a narrow loss, the province's premier Jacques Parizeau infuriated the nation when he blamed the ethnic vote for the defeat. Parizeau made no bones about it when asked to clarify his statements later. In a 2013 interview he said, "I knew very well who I was targeting when I said that—the common front of Italian, Greek, and Jewish congresses."

While independence supporters in Quebec typically don't openly display the sort of bigotry Parizeau did, they do see the presence of immigrants as an obstacle in their path to independence. It's why they create legislation like the controversial Bill 21 that bans the display of any religious adornment by public employees and it's why they bring in other ridiculous laws like Bill 101 so Chinese restaurants can be fined for displaying signs in Chinese. People who wear turbans, hijabs, and kippahs aren't typically supporters of French-speaking nationalism so the independence supporters in Quebec's government have been engaged in a long-term campaign to make those Quebecers feel as uncomfortable as possible in the province. It's a vulgar display of legislative intolerance and the deafening silence from federal leaders demonstrates the stranglehold Quebec has on Canada's federal politicians.

I don't for one second want to see the West engage in such a repugnant campaign to create preferential referendum conditions such as Quebec is doing. We need to reach out and be inclusive rather than exclusive. Western independence is about freedom-loving individuals, no matter what language they might want to speak or what religion they adhere to. While linguistic unity provides Quebec with an easy, unifying base of support for their independence movement, it also pushes them into intolerance of diversity and weakens their movement in a much broader sense. As long as western independence remains focused on diversity and inclusiveness among supporters, it will build a stronger base of support than Quebec can ever dream of. Many of the most dedicated supporters for western independence come from other parts of the world and we would be fools not to welcome them.

We ought to be appealing to and drawing in those people from linguistic and religious minorities who are oppressed within Quebec and we should be inviting them out west. They would bring a valuable and skilled labour pool to the West's economy and would relish the individual freedoms the West offers that Quebec doesn't. In other words, these folks are potentially ideal supporters of western independence. Like the rest of us, they just want the freedom to live life in the way of their choosing and the opportunity to work hard and prosper.

Foundation for the win

The lesson Quebec does offer is one on willingness to bide their time to create winning conditions for referendum success.

If we want to set western independence back a decade, all we need to do is hold a premature referendum, then lose the vote. Interest in independence will wane and the federalists will claim a solid mandate to maintain the status quo in favour of Central Canada.

Until we're confident of a strong victory, we shouldn't move towards a referendum. In some ways, a narrow win in an independence referendum would be as bad as a loss. It would invite doubt and conspiracy claims about the integrity of the referendum process and it would drag out negotiations while federalists try to undo the results. Just look how painful the process of Brexit has been in the UK despite a successful vote—by a thin margin—to leave the EU.

We need to set our sights on holding a single referendum with a strong support base and winning a decisive vote for independence. Technically, 50 percent plus one might be enough to win secession, but we should strive for no less than 60 percent. We must not leave room for doubt about the results of the vote.

The Clarity Act requires a "clear majority" in an independence referendum. That's an ambiguous statement and it's open to interpretation. We can be sure anything less than 60 percent support for independence in a referendum will be immediately challenged in Canadian courts. We need to strive for a strong and conclusive win.

While contemporary support for independence can spike between 20 and 25 percent, that number will drop in a referendum when push comes to shove. It's a solid base to build from, but it's nowhere near the level of support we need to secede.

Our task as ambassadors for independence is to identify our support base and engage those people. With their attention, we can work to expand support. We need to find those who are currently passive in their support for independence and turn them into people who actively advocate for it.

Walking the talk

So, if it's not yet time for a referendum, what's the first thing we need to do? The answer is simple: we must lead by example.

It can't be overemphasized that western provinces must clean up their own acts before any independence movement can be taken seriously. How can we promote the benefits of independence when our own governments are no better than the feds? Has your provincial government balanced its budget? Has there been democratic reform? Does it have a supportive pro-business environment? Are taxes reasonable? How about the protections of individual rights?

In the province of Alberta, for example, the government is presently a catastrophe. The health care system is in shambles, discontent is rampant, and for decades no progress towards provincial autonomy has been pursued, let alone accomplished. Municipalities are battling the provincial government, and former premier Jason Kenney was tossed from leadership by his own party.

With that mess in mind, how can Albertans keep a straight face when trying to convince folks the province would be better off on its own?

I have two words to calm down overly exuberant Albertan independence supporters who yearn for an immediate referendum: "President Notley." Alberta once elected a socialist New Democratic Party (NDP) government and might very well do so again. While that's damaging enough for a province, imagine how bad it would be for a nation. We need to get our population united and not make a bad situation worse.

Saskatchewan, Manitoba, and BC have all elected NDP governments at one time or another. It will take years of responsible governance at a provincial level before people consider independence a superior option to the current national agreement.

It's easy to point to the flaws in federal governance. It's harder to make the case that an independent province would be any better off if its own government doesn't have a commendable track record.

Our provinces must change how they do things and should evolve in the direction of autonomy. We don't need to look for fights with Ottawa, we'll find them soon enough when our provinces begin asserting and distancing themselves from federal control. Those battles will help entrench support for independence, but again, people need to have faith that their province is strong and can govern itself well. That's a starting point.

There's very little we can do in order to change or improve the federal government in Canada, we know that. It's why we're promoting independence. There's a lot we can and must do provincially before we can claim the high ground and promote secession. We must convince a majority of citizens in each western province that independence is in their best interests. We won't be able to do it if provinces' governments are inept. I'm confident the West can lead by example, but we need to find the will and the means to do so.

When a provincial government is acting in the best interest of citizens but is stymied by Ottawa, people will truly realize how essential independence is. When Alberta demonstrates economic and fiscal responsibility, the federal government works harder to drain us. When Saskatchewan refuses to play ball with federal gun-grabs, the RCMP steps in on Ottawa's behalf. When Manitoba's agricultural sector is productive and efficient, the federal government offers fertilizer bans. When BC builds a liquified natural gas port for exports and activists block the pipeline, the federal government sits on its hands.

Strong provincial governments will always butt heads with the federal government because western interests don't serve Ottawa's interests. Those clashes are what will create winning referendum conditions. First, we need to create those strong provincial governments. We need to get involved with and influence our political parties to create the environment we need to move forward on independence.

Chapter 7

AMBASSADORS FOR INDEPENDENCE

In December of 1980, the *Globe and Mail* described western separatism as "primitive and confused, groping for a platform and searching for a leader." Here we are over forty years later and the statement is as true as ever. Leaders have come and gone alongside parties that have proposed a myriad of policies and initiatives.

Western independence is the right goal. It's the only way we can break free from a system designed to exploit us. We know the solution to the problem, but we have been pursuing it the wrong way.

Before any leader, party, or organization can establish a long-term presence, there needs to be a solid base of support for independence for them to stand upon. There is a role for leaders, organizations, and parties, but the time for them is not upon us yet.

As the old adage goes: "If you want something done right, do it yourself."

Organizations and parties are important and by all means join and support them. However, be aware those groups are prone to becoming echo chambers and that you will be spending time preaching to the converted among them. What the independence movement needs are newly minted supporters of western independence. As an independence advocate, you must engage people while they are upset and direct them to the solution. Their ire won't last, and they will sink back into dejection and apathy if they aren't directed to a productive outlet. Your role is to get them there.

Western independence won't happen thanks to a group, party, or leader. The foundation for independence begins with the efforts of countless individuals, not organizations. Take up the cause as a personal mandate, not to the point of being an annoying fanatic, of course, but you must always be ready to build the movement at every opportunity.

You're an ambassador for independence. You represent the movement and you're no less able to do so than any public leader or policy maker. You have a role and it's an important one. It comes with responsibility. A poor ambassador can do more damage to the cause than good. You must have a goal and a plan and take the role seriously and pursue it relentlessly.

Whether at the workplace, on social media, at a seat in the pub, or at a family gathering, you are on duty. Those are your opportunities to reach new people and to bring them on board. Approach carefully, though, or you can also become a social pariah. Diplomacy means knowing when to get into the issues and when to leave them at the door.

Understand that while a growing number of people are realizing our current system of Confederation is failing, they aren't necessarily ready to dive into a push for independence.

Your communication regarding independence should be measured and planned. You must try to be patient and polite (not always easy, in my experience).

OK, you're ready to engage someone. They are receptive to some political chat and you have read this book cover to cover, of course. You are overflowing with answers, stats, salient points, and counterpoints. A recent issue between Ottawa and the West has primed the pump and you have a potential convert to the independence cause.

How do you break the ice? I believe the best way is with a question-and-thought exercise. Have you ever had a stubborn boss who would only embrace a notion if they were convinced it was their own idea? You lead them through a series of questions that bring them to the conclusion you want. This sounds almost deceptive, but it really isn't. It's just speeding them through the personal question-and-answer process—the same drawn-out process that likely made you a supporter of independence in the first place, only this is the condensed version.

The question goes something like this: If the West was independent of Canada today—a sovereign state—would you support re-joining with Canada under our current arrangement?

If a person firmly believes the West is presently getting a good deal and nothing needs to change in the agreement, there is little to be gained in discussing independence further with them. Switch the topic to sports or something else uncontroversial. There is no sense losing friendships over intransigence. Be patient. It may just be the wrong time. Future events might change a person's perspective and you can approach them on the issue later.

Most people, however, would be able to name at least a few things they would change if they were negotiating a merger with Canada. These are seeds you can plant and foster with them. There are plenty to choose from. Topics include equalization, the Senate, federal seat distribution, property rights, resource control, democratic reform, health policies, and free speech, to name a few. And the list goes on.

Once you've established a few things in need of change in order to build a new Confederation, you will likely find almost all those amendments would require reworking Canada's Constitution Act as a first step.

Breaking up is hard to do. Or is it?

The last serious efforts to change the Constitution were the Meech Lake and Charlottetown Accords of the early 1990s. Both attempts to amend the Constitution failed and nobody has made any real efforts to change it since. Politicians and activists entrenched themselves in the idea that constitutional reform is unlikely within Canada, so they avoid the issue when possible.

Amending the Constitution is no easy affair, nor should it be. A constitution is what defines the entire policy framework of a nation. It should not and cannot be changed on a whim. Unfortunately, the process for amending Canada's Constitution makes it almost impossible to substantially alter the document.

If indeed the Constitution were to be amended, it's unlikely those changes would benefit the West without the substantial influence of those who represent western interests. It requires the House of Commons, the Senate and seven provincial legislatures to comprise 50 percent of the country's population in order to amend the Constitution, or it gives all power to Ontario and Quebec, as has historically been the case. Those provinces will never support constitutional changes that empower provinces beyond Central Canada.

A flawed system that can't be fixed from within leaves you with two choices: You either quit fighting and struggle on, or you pursue regional independence to achieve change. If Central Canada were ever to consider constitutional changes that would benefit the West, it would mean a province or region was seriously on the cusp of secession. And that requires a solid and stable independence movement.

If a person can come up with a realistic third option in that discussion, please send it my way, because it has always eluded me.

This discussion may not create an instant independence supporter, but it never fails to get a person thinking about the stalemate we seem to be in. Nothing short of a unity crisis—where a province is on the brink of a positive independence referendum vote, or has held a positive independence referendum vote—will inspire enough of the nation to get constitutional changes successfully ratified. At that point, either the West separates, or a new deal is negotiated.

Don't give up on someone if they don't initially seem enthusiastic with the idea. It's difficult to know what they might conclude if given time. Once, while setting up a booth at a sportsman's show with the Alberta Independence Party, a fellow approached me and barraged me with questions. He was abrupt but pointed and spent fifteen minutes interrogating me. He walked away without saying anything and I thought, "Well, there's one person who will never support us." A week later, and much to my surprise, he showed up at one of our town hall meetings and cut us a sizeable cheque. He became a dedicated party supporter. He just needed time to think about it and come to his own conclusions.

Social Media

You have many tools at your disposal to promote independence and they should all be used responsibly. Social media is a good example. Think of it as a power tool.

Individuals and groups have more avenues of communication at their disposal than at any time in history. The realm of social media is an essential space for independence proponents. It enables us to bypass the biased establishment media. We can debate, organize, and share ideas at virtually no cost. We have the potential to reach out directly to millions of people at little or no expense.

While social media is one of the most powerful tools a citizen has at their disposal, it can also be the most destructive. Anyone can use social media but not everybody is good at it, and it shows.

A brilliant one-line statement or meme from the most unexpected of people can take off and go viral online. A social media post casually tapped out on a cellphone has the potential to reach thousands or perhaps millions of people. It's not necessarily a good thing. A post that seemed profound or inspired at the time might be taken out of context and look crass to your social media audience. Hell let's face it, the post may even be plain stupid, we all have our moments. This kind of post can seriously undermine a movement or campaign. And we must never forget, things posted to the internet remain there forever. You can quickly delete an "Oh shit" moment from your Twitter timeline upon realizing it wasn't such a wise tweet, but you can rest assured someone has already saved it and that it will be shared later—and often—at the worst possible time for you. Be principled, disciplined, and discerning about everything you post on social media, whether it's Facebook, Twitter, Snapchat, or even the lesser used platforms like Locals and Steemit. There are more than 133 contemporary social media platforms and the potential exists for a serious mistake on any of them and the error could be equally as damaging as any indiscretion on Twitter.

Try to keep an internet version of Miranda rights in mind before sharing something: Anything you say can and will be used against you in court of law—in this case, the court of public opinion.

Posting while hot-headed or drunk can often lead to disaster. I haven't had a drink in years, but I have to be mindful not to indulge my anger, however. I rarely write notions of brilliance when I have a head of steam on an issue. Anger can inspire action but try to cool down a little, or a lot, before going public. These tips should be applied to your social media conduct outside of the political realm, too. All your expression in public reflects on you and your position as a proponent of western independence.

All those warnings aside, social media is a fantastic tool. Promoting a concept or organizing groups has never been easier. We need to use social media effectively if we want to create a tipping point of support for independence. Just look at how hard authoritarians in Ottawa are trying to control the flow of information on social media. They know how powerful online information sharing and public political debate is and how it has the potential to threaten the status quo.

Social media is a complicated, algorithm-based world. Algorithms greatly influence which posts go viral and which don't. We can help pro-independence messaging rise to the top even with the most passive of participation.

In order to be most effective, don't be anonymous if you can help it. I understand some people fear workplace reprisals and have good reason to maintain anonymous accounts on social media. When a post or discussion on social media comes from an account clearly representing a real person, it carries far more weight than an anonymous post. Readers understand it is a genuine individual behind the keyboard and will take posts more seriously. They want to know they are engaging with other folks like themselves and not some bot generated by a bored person in their basement, or one of thousands from an offshore industrial bot farm. Bots and fake accounts are a scourge on social media channels and users have trained themselves to ignore anonymous posts.

Think of it like election campaign signs. During every election, public spaces become so polluted with candidates' signs they pretty much become 'white noise' to those who look at them. People see the signs but the names don't register. When a campaign sign appears on a person's lawn, it's a different matter. It indicates a person has made a conscious decision about a candidate, platform, or issue and wants to openly display their point of view. It shows commitment, even if minor, and it will have an impact on neighbours and others who see the sign, even on a subconscious level. No number of signs on the side of a public roadway will convince a person how to vote, but if most of their neighbours have the same signs on their lawn, it's impactful. Humans are herd animals by nature. People on social media behave much the same way and therefore those who put their name behind their messaging will naturally be more likely to influence others.

You can take a more passive approach online and still contribute to the independence cause. You don't have to write, debate, or take part directly in the social media arena. Just be sure to subscribe to, like, and share posts and accounts promoting independence. There's a reason social media influencers are always nagging you to like and share channels and posts—they do it because it works.

The more likes and shares a social media post can garner, the more likely it is the platform will automatically promote the post. Getting articles and videos trending is golden and you never know just which posts will take off. If you don't help get the ball rolling via those initial likes and shares, though, the post might languish unseen in its own little corner of the internet.

In 2016, I posted a short video of myself opening a fossil concretion at an Alberta mine and didn't think much of it. It tripped a YouTube algorithm and went viral. The video has now amassed over 1.4 million views. Thankfully, it wasn't a clip of me doing something embarrassing. Treat every post as if it might go viral.

Getting into the nitty gritty of internet debate is great, too, but like everything else, it must be done with care. The most important and difficult lesson of all is to learn to give someone else the last word. Twitter is my preferred social media playground and I have managed to acquire tens of thousands of followers. It's a great platform for promoting articles and quick thoughts. It's not a good spot for extended debates. If you want to reduce your follower count, there are few better ways to do so than to get into a prolonged fight with someone online. No one wants to read an extended back-and-forth between two people with intractable positions for hours or days. People will tune out and eventually unfollow you. It took me a while to figure that one out. Either let them have the last word after a short exchange or block them.

Yes, blocking is an essential tool in the social media toolbox. You are not infringing on anyone's right to free speech if you block them on social media, though they may howl that you are. Everyone is as free as they've ever been to spout whatever they want. They just don't have the right to do it on your social media feeds. If you let a person continue to highjack your discussion, you are letting them steal your stage. If it were a public discussion, it would be the same as letting them take your microphone while you were mid-speech. Everyone has the right to free speech, but you are not obliged to share your podium with them.

On Twitter you have an option to mute people. They can still tweet away at you, but you will no longer see their tweets. I used to think that was a good idea but later realized it wasn't. When you mute people, you give them the ability to derail the entire thread of a discussion and you won't even know it's happened. If you have identified a person as being disruptive or trolling on social media, block them without hesitation. You will never bring those trolls over to your point of view. They will drag you away from the point you're making and into the mire, and they'll do it at every opportunity. Don't let them waste your time and steal your platform.

When engaging in debate online, try to look at it as a moderated election debate. You can make a point, then someone else can make a rebuttal, and perhaps you offer one more response. If you go beyond that, your discourse becomes a fruitless argument and your point is lost. Someone vociferously opposed to independence might never be convinced by the opposite argument, but many people viewing your discussion could be sitting on the fence. They will lose interest if the discussion turns into a long, circular battle. Fight the urge to respond and move on to something else. Block the respondent if they won't let it go.

Avoid spamming people. If someone posts about Aunt Maggie's 90th birthday, don't jump in and point out how much better her birthday would be in an independent West. Don't relentlessly message or email people with independence posts, even if you mean well. You will find yourself being blocked and worst of all, you might harm friendships and family relationships. Take politics seriously, but never take it personally. Not everybody wants to hear what you have to share and it's not worth the cost of a valuable relationship. I can't stress this enough. Many people have given up on politics due to having so many fights and taking on too much personal stress over the issues. Often, they just needed to learn when to step back a bit.

Post cute kitten videos and funny memes now and then. Being too damn serious all the time will drive people away from your social media feed as fast as belligerence will.

There is much well-founded mistrust of the social media giants amongst users. The algorithmic bias demonstrated by Facebook and Twitter is hard to miss. That said, most people spend time on at least one of those major platforms every day, and they need to be reached. Some have retreated to alternative platforms such as Gab or Rumble. Those platforms have value but are often echo chambers where meaningful debate is mostly absent. If you want to convert folks to the cause, you will need to venture forth into the more mainstream social media platforms, whether you like it or not.

Get out and use social media. Share those great memes. Write those blog posts and share those Facebook thoughts. It's all part of the way we'll be able to incrementally build the support base we need for independence. Just do it with careful thought and foresight. You're an ambassador for independence. Always act on that premise.

A little shameless self-promotion on social media doesn't hurt either. Be sure to share links to this book, for example, via every social media channel you have. This could be the handbook we've all been waiting for!

Taking on the legacy media

While social media is beginning to dominate communication and the dissemination of information, the mainstream news media networks and agencies are still there. You might sometimes find yourself engaged with them. The legacy media is a dinosaur, possibly on the path to extinction. It's hopelessly biased and is becoming increasingly dependent on government funding, if it isn't entirely dependent, already. CBC News is possibly the worst of those outlets while broadcasters like CTV and Global fare little better.

The ways the legacy media slants the narrative can be devious and subtle. To use a good example, newsrooms and newspapers made scant efforts to avoid bias during the truckers' Freedom Convoy protests in Ottawa early in 2022.

While much of it is still worth watching—they have the broadest networks on the ground for now—one has to watch assiduously the way they package the messaging. Notice how they use the camera lighting on people they like versus those they don't. Is the camera angle looking up towards them to make them look dominant, or is it slightly angled downward to diminish them? These are subtle ways a news department can venture into opinion.

The CBC taught me a hard lesson when I was heading the Alberta Independence Party in 2001. I was invited to do a segment on *Newsworld* at the CBC Calgary headquarters. I wasn't unaware of the bias at the CBC, but we couldn't avoid participating with the broadcaster at the time. At this point, online alternative news media was all but non-existent.

After passing through security in the building, I was led into a large, bustling newsroom. Off to one side, a green screen and camera had been set up with a small wooden stool in front. The producer was congenial enough as he wired me up with a lapel microphone and earpiece. He said I would soon hear from the producer in Toronto via my earpiece when it was time to go live. He proceeded to abandon me perched atop a horribly uncomfortable stool.

People walked back and forth on each side of my little pop-up studio. I was inexperienced and stressed. I only got more nervous and uncomfortable as the minutes dragged by. I was probably sitting there for ten minutes or so, but it felt like hours. A voice popped into my ear telling me we were going live in two minutes. By then I was a wreck.

I muddled my way through a ten-minute interview by the end of which I was drenched in sweat. People watching it must have wondered why

Cory Morgan seemed so twitchy, nervous, and distracted. They had no idea I was sitting on a hard stool in the middle of an open concept office hub.

I have since done interviews in the same building and been taken into one of the many studios they have. It is conceivable they simply didn't have space available in one of the studios at the time. I find it hard to believe, though, and I doubt they'd have hosted a senior politician or guest that way. It was a clever and subtle way to ensure I wasn't on my best game for the interview.

That said, the mainstream media is still very influential, and we can't afford to ignore them. They might be fading in relevance, but still, they reach millions of westerners on a daily basis. We gained more members and donors after my CBC interview. The piece reached people who'd been previously out of reach, despite my awkwardness on set. Refusing to engage with the mainstream media leaves too many potential supporters under the radar. You can respond to the mainstream media, and it can be productive. Keep this in mind: if you refuse to speak to a reporter, they might move on to someone who could say something that hurts the cause for independence. Your having given them a reasonable clip can prevent this undesirable outcome.

I watched a Calgary newscast during the height of the COVID-19 pandemic protests that demonstrated well how some activists harm their own cause through their distrust of the media.

The top news item was about a few small groups of people who had attended protests at UCP constituency offices. They had put childish chalk drawings on the sidewalks outside and taped paper notes to the doors of the offices. It appeared there were no more than five or six people at each office and it really was not an impressive showing. They had about seven minutes of coverage on the evening news, however, and several of the protesters were interviewed. Their little ragtag demonstration reached the living rooms of tens of thousands of viewers.

Conversely, in the next segment of the broadcast, a Calgary march attended by thousands protesting pandemic restrictions received no more than ten seconds of coverage. So how do we account for the difference in coverage between the two events?

It could be argued some of it was media bias against the Calgary marchers. The establishment simply isn't fond of them. It might also be said the two demonstrations were organized differently and differed in the way each responded to media coverage.

Those protesting outside of the constituency offices were union-backed. They were few, but organized. The media didn't just stumble across these guys. There would have been a press release. When reporters arrived, I expect they weren't terribly impressed with the turnout. The crew had made the trip and they still needed to provide news content. They interviewed multiple people and created plenty of footage. The demonstrators also welcomed their attention.

The marchers probably didn't issue any information to the media—decentralized leadership can have its disadvantages. If you want coverage for an event, it never hurts to send a heads-up to media outlets. They need content to fill their broadcasts and websites and if you make it easy for them, they will often indulge you. The other problem is anti-restriction protesters are frequently hostile to the legacy media—they won't talk to them or can even be aggressive towards them. It's little wonder they didn't merit much coverage in the evening news. You don't have to like reporters from the legacy media outlets, but you should treat them courteously.

The media may not always be favourable to your cause, but they often can be. If you treat them with respect, you can at least reduce the chances of negative coverage. If you are shouting and swearing at them, you can almost guarantee a negative report, that's if they cover your event at all. There are still some genuinely unbiased reporters out there who just want to file the story. There is little to be lost in using some diplomacy when dealing with the press.

Kid gloves and savoir faire

When you engage people in person or online, you must be tactful and polite while in the role of independence ambassador. Tact and diplomacy is effective. It's the product of being cognizant of the feelings of those with whom you're engaging. The emotional case against independence may appear pointless, but it is real.

Sentiment and emotions are consequential and they determine our actions and objectives. Instinctively, we group ourselves in families, local communities, and, more broadly, as nations. As groups, we share traditions and take pride in our histories. We bond and we enjoy the connection with all other Canadians, regardless of region. The case for independence must be made carefully and sensitively so we can still enjoy all those feelings and have that sense of connection even when—and I say that optimistically—the West becomes independent.

Canada is a vast nation comprising several regions held together by contract, nothing more. In seeking western independence, it must be understood we're aiming to renegotiate a contract. It's not disloyal to seek to amend a contract that no longer serves our interests. It doesn't mean we hate our neighbours if we want to live under a different system of governance than theirs. It certainly isn't treason, yet one who pursues western independence can be and will be accused of these things by those who want to protect the status quo. Those accusations can hurt and that's the intent of those who throw them around.

We must let those kinds of accusations slide and refuse to retaliate. In doing this, we keep the debate in the rational realm and we maintain credibility. Antagonizing political opponents whether they're local or out East will not serve our cause. Resist the temptation to do so.

Divorce is never an easy process. As much as we're convinced the time has come to part ways, feelings of attachment still remain. When we let those feelings overcome our reason, we might say and do things that harm and hinder a process that requires rationale. We—or at least most of us—don't hate Canada. We have simply concluded our relationship cannot continue as it stands and are working to redefine it. While it's difficult, a separation can happen where both parties are happy in the long run and can still maintain a civil relationship.

To see how a post-secession relationship can work, we need only look to Europe for examples.
Sweden and Norway held a very close relationship as separate kingdoms for centuries with many ups and downs. They formed their last official union in in 1814 as the United Kingdoms of Sweden and Norway under Charles XIII. As close nations with very similar cultures, a union appeared feasible, though unification was messy. While each nation still enjoyed its own constitution and parliament—providing some regional autonomy—Sweden's larger population led to a lopsided union as the monarch resided predominantly in Sweden. Foreign policies were modelled to protect Sweden's interests, often at the expense of Norway's economic interests. As tensions grew, so did fear of war between the nations. In a 1905 plebiscite, Norwegians voted overwhelmingly in favour of independence, and the result was the independent constitutional monarchy of Norway.

There were tensions between Norway and Sweden both before and after the dissolution of their union. There can be no doubt there were strong feelings and broken hearts. The countries had been closely intertwined for generations. Separating was no simple thing, yet it happened, and it happened peacefully. Today, both nations enjoy their autonomy while retaining their close relationship. No passport is required for travel between them, and their trading relationship is very tight. They are independent nations with stability and prosperity that are the envy of the world. The two nations are better off as closely tied but independent neighbours than they ever had been under a union. That's because they took the rational approach and separated from each other amicably when the relationship broke down.

A more contemporary example of an amicable separation is the Czech Republic and Slovakia—formerly Czechoslovakia. While mashed together as Czechoslovakia under the umbrella of the Soviet Union for nearly seventy years, the two nations quickly separated when the Soviet empire collapsed. The dissolution of Czechoslovakia is often referred to as the Velvet Divorce due to its peaceful and warmly negotiated manner. Again, two closely related cultures living within one nation managed to peacefully divide into two distinct and independent nations and still retain strong ties and a healthy relationship.

There is no reason Canada can't achieve this kind of relationship of two autonomous states while maintaining close trade and cultural ties.

The mind will look to the circumstances of Confederation and support western independence. The heart, however, can overwhelm the mind and move a yes vote to a no vote in a referendum. It's part of why support for secession is much greater in the polls than it is in an election result with an independence option on the ballot. When the rubber hits the road, sentiment often wins.

If we want to achieve western independence, we will need to win both the hearts and minds of supporters. This will take time, careful discourse, and sensitivity to the feelings of those who still feel a strong attachment to the concept of Confederation. Reason will win in the end, but it must be applied gently and intelligently.

Canada will still exist the day after a positive vote for western independence. The terms between regions will have changed and we will all be the better for it in the long run.

Immigration is an asset not a liability

Immigrants built the West and remain essential to its future. A referendum on western independence will never win unless a large segment of newcomers to the West supports it. Whether incoming from other nations or other provinces, new westerners are often very receptive to the idea of western independence.

Western independence groups will have to become more supportive of newcomers if they want them to get on board. Not only should you be supportive of new westerners, but you also need to call people out who show intolerance towards them. I am not talking about embracing open borders and abandoning immigration control in an independent West, but it must be understood that existing and new immigrants are essential for the West's prosperity. Alienating newcomers is counterproductive, to say the least.

I can't count the number of times I've heard people telling me, "We will go Liberal in Alberta soon if we don't stop immigration!" or, "Non-born Albertans will never support independence!"

Both presumptions are wrong and we have solid numbers to prove it.

Alberta has long been considered the most conservative-minded province in Canada. During most of its history, Alberta, along with the rest of the West, has seen large spurts of population growth due to immigration. Alberta's population has nearly doubled since 1980 and has grown from three million people to over four million between 2001 and 2016. If migration to Alberta were to turn the province liberal, it would have happened decades ago.

Support for independence has been growing steadily for decades. Newcomers are not as averse to supporting change as some might think.

The West was and remains something of a frontier. People relocate so they can build a future here. It takes a lot of courage, ambition, and strength for someone to leave their family, friends, and support networks to take a chance in a new country or province. People who choose to move to Western Canada are individualists who want to guide their own future. They don't expect the government to take care of them. This is true whether we speak of the tough pioneers who broke ground in the West well over a century ago or the present-day immigrants from around the world seeking new careers and opportunities. Newcomers to the West are rarely liberals and they are potentially ideal supporters of independence.

New westerners are often the most upset when they see government incursions interfering with their goals for prosperity and individual freedoms. Westerners who originated in the Maritime provinces know very well how destructive Canada's regional policies have been on the economy and the regional pride of the East Coast. Immigrants from Eastern Europe remember clearly how their regions suffered under a distant, central government in Moscow prior to the dissolution of the USSR. Venezuelan immigrants witnessed how socialism can destroy countries blessed with even the most abundant of resources. And Chinese immigrants know how miserable it is to live under an authoritarian state. None of these incoming westerners want to see their new homeland become akin to the one they managed to escape. They are the best allies of independence movements when they are confident independence means protection against that from which they fled.

The greater threat to independence comes from homegrown citizens who have become indoctrinated to believe big government is their friend. Many born westerners are spoiled and have a deep sense of entitlement. They don't see the longer-term threat to their wellbeing as those from other regions and don't realize we need to be proactive to maintain and protect our freedoms and prosperity. Think of it this way, Rachel Notley was born and raised in Alberta—being western-born doesn't necessarily mean one is a good westerner.

We need to embrace new westerners and foster support among them. Let's help them integrate and have them share our pride as westerners. Everyone in the West is descended from an immigrant of one kind or another if we go back far enough. Immigration made the region strong and will continue to do so. We will not see a successful referendum outcome for independence without a significant level of support from new westerners, so let's ensure we don't make the mistake of alienating them.

Party tricks and playbooks

This is an expression I often hear and it makes me cringe: "Separation if necessary, but not necessarily separation."

The phrase was adopted during the founding convention of the Alberta Independence Party. I explain at length in this book why I feel overtly secessionist parties are not the way to go in the pursuit of independence for the West. That said, if you're bluffing in your own mission statement, you have neutered yourself.

The federal Maverick Party was created from the Wexit Party. Wexit unreservedly pursued independence and gained fast support. The Mavericks will struggle to remain relevant if they don't embrace a serious pursuit of western independence, but they won't be able to gain a large amount of popular support if they remain focused on independence. It's an impossible balancing act to maintain and it's why parties themselves are of limited use to the independence movement.

The Maverick Party serves an important role as a pro-western voice. They will always be pushed back and forth, however, between supporting full independence and talking around it. I hope they remain on the scene and build to a point where they can put some pressure on Conservative Party of Canada members in the West. They have a tough row to hoe.

An unapologetic western-based party on the federal scene is very useful. Some of the best federal governance we've ever seen in Canada was by the Liberal Party with the Reform Party in opposition breathing down its neck. In Parliament, the Bloc Québécois is an effective advocate for Quebec interests. The Bloc will never form government, and it's not their intention to do so. The status quo allows them to remain focused on their regional priorities. They seem to have found the sweet spot of being a regional party without being overtly secessionist. Perhaps the Maverick Party will find that sweet spot, too.

I have heard from many people that we should use the threat of secessionism as a bargaining chip. They say we should be just like Quebec in that sense. They are wrong on both fronts.

When I led the Alberta Independence Party, I had the opportunity to meet with some representatives of Quebec's Bloc Québécois. One thing I took away from those meetings is that these people were deadly serious in their pursuit of full independence for Quebec. They knew full well it would be economically damaging if the province left the Confederation, but they didn't care. They were true secessionists. If the government were to offer Quebec incentives to stay, the Bloc and Parti Québécois were more than happy to take them. However, it didn't make them want their independent nation any less.

The reason Quebec gets constant concessions from Ottawa is the players in Ottawa know damn well the independence movement in Quebec is very real. It may be on the back burner right now, but it can and likely will flare into a crisis again, soon. Remember, the margin of the last independence referendum in Quebec was razor thin and, yes, they knew what they were voting for. Rest assured if Ottawa thought Quebec was bluffing, the constant pandering would be tempered, to say the least.

For the West to say we want to use the threat of independence to get our way with Ottawa is akin to playing poker with your cards facing your opponent. Ottawa will only fear the western independence movement if it has teeth. They will need to see regional polling that demonstrates growing support for independence and its proponents remaining intractable. If we don't mean it, it all means nothing.

Don't let people water things down. Don't set conditions for the West remaining within Confederation. At best, this only puts off the inevitable. The system is broken. No short-term policy changes or concessions will change that. Separation is necessary. Leave it at that.

Suicidal politics—extremists and mavericks

Few things can sink a movement faster than the voice of a lunatic fringe. Smaller movements will always draw extreme folk with extreme ideas. There are people with crazy notions who will try to latch onto a new movement to use it as a platform. That's unavoidable. While these people always make up a tiny minority among the supporters of a cause, they tend to be maddeningly vocal and can cause terrible damage. What's important is how the movement deals with these voices.

Opponents of western independence relish finding a campaign crackpot they can use to smear the movement. They will gleefully showcase whatever crazy or offensive views the person promoted and will try to tar and feather the entire movement with it. This has been done since the beginning of political movements because it's devastatingly effective. When a group or movement is spending as much time explaining or apologizing for things their fringe supporters have said, they have already lost the argument.

Conservative-minded people tend to hold free speech as a sacred principle. I do, too. It must be understood, though, being obligated to support free speech does not mean everyone gets a platform. Banning someone with controversial views from the mic at meetings is not a free speech infringement. That person has every right to say whatever they please, they just have to say it elsewhere. A movement cannot afford to let fringe activists derail the cause. And it must carefully manage every public speaking environment

I was a campaign manager for one of the Wildrose Party candidates during the 2012 Alberta general election. One night, it was revealed on social media a party candidate had archaic and offensive opinions when it came to the LGBTQ+ community. On Twitter, I began loudly decrying those candidate's views and got into an argument with some of the Wildrose candidates. My phone soon rang. I was asked by one of the Wildrose Party campaign co-chairs to back off. They assured me they had the situation under control. I complied, and watched, and waited. They failed and let it get out of hand.

Danielle Smith was the party leader at the time, and she declined to strongly condemn the candidate or to remove his party endorsement. She was in an awfully difficult position. As a supporter of free speech and the independence of caucus members, she was loath to intervene on a candidate's views or his right to express them. At the same time, the wider population was mortified and consequently the issue persisted.

Eventually, Smith tried to compromise on the issue and failed. The Wildrose Party had been leading in the polls, but support collapsed.

Urban candidates were wiped out on Election Day and Alison Redford was re-elected as Alberta's premier despite having run a lousy campaign.

Albertans were ready to vote for change and put the Wildrose Party in power, but their support was tentative and fragile. The Wildrose Party was new and that can make people nervous. Without a track record in government, it can be tough for a new party to assure voters they don't hold a hidden, extreme agenda. At the first whiff of potential extremism, support for the Wildrose evaporated.

Always remember, while support for independence is growing, that support is fragile. At this point it's a lot easier to push people away from the movement than to it is to draw them in.

The window of time the Wildrose Party had to deal with the wayward candidate was well before the election. His thoughts on the LGBTQ community had been documented a year before they surfaced at election time. The party should have weeded him out long before the election hit. A movement needs to be proactive rather than reactive when dealing with candidates with extremist views. What was to become known as the Hunsperger scandal blew up a week before voting day in Alberta. There was nothing Danielle Smith could have done by then to prevent the damage it caused by then. Somebody had found Hunsperger's blog posting well before the election and saved it for strategic use. They released it just before the election to cause maximum damage to the Wildrose Party campaign and leave them with little time to recover from it. Similar actions will be conducted by opponents to independence when the time for a referendum campaign comes. One can't account for every possibility but advocates for independence shouldn't make it easy for their opponents either.

When the time comes for an independence referendum, federalists will be doing everything in their power to paint the movement as extreme. While that's unfair, it's also inevitable. We must avoid making it easy for them by providing ready targets in the form of radical voices. Condemn fringe elements quickly and firmly, or they will derail us.

There must be a zero-tolerance policy when it comes to extreme views. Racism, religious fundamentalism, and general bigotry mustn't be tolerated. They have nothing to do with the pursuit of independence and it must stay that way.

During the Freedom Convoy protests in Ottawa, two isolated incidents gave convoy opponents ammunition to portray protest participants as racists. Both examples involved flags. One was a person who walked among the protesters carrying an American Confederate flag and the other flag was a Nazi swastika. Prime Minister Justin Trudeau and the establishment media never let up on the presence of those flags. Trudeau even accused a Jewish member of Parliament of standing with Nazis.

The Nazi flag was never actually seen in the protest itself. Despite thousands of people with cameras documenting the protests, only two pictures of the odious flag were ever seen. In fact, the person with the flag never actually joined the protests. That situation reeked of a set-up perpetrated by protest opponents—a real false flag event—and there really is little to be done to defend against it, except eject offenders in the moment, where possible. It does demonstrate the lengths to which anti-freedom advocates will go, though, and independence advocates will always need to be on guard for such attempts to sabotage the movement from within.

The person with the Confederate flag did walk among the protesters for a short period of time. He was the only 'protester' wearing a full-face mask, which by itself brought his motives into immediate question. Some good came of that flag incident, however. Protesters very quickly made it clear the flag-bearer and his message were not welcome. Video was taken showing protesters driving the man out from their midst and it was shared widely on social media. It was the best defense the protesters could have against that one man's actions. They visibly demonstrated he didn't represent them and they told him to get the hell away.

I did see some naive fools trying to explain how the flag doesn't necessarily represent racism. Symbols are powerful, they're important, their meaning evolves, and context matters, as well as location. There simply is no context where the US Confederate flag should be waved at a Canadian protest. If you spend time making excuses or explaining why the flag isn't a problem, you've already lost whatever message you were trying to convey. Just avoid the problem in the first place. Building support for western independence will involve discussion on many controversial topics, we need not add American politics to the mix.

In Edmonton during protests against the COVID-19 mask mandates, a handful of idiots decided that marching down the streets while holding lit tiki torches would be a good idea. This is an example of how symbols change. Prior to 2017, marching with tiki torches in a protest would have meant nothing. Since some actual neo-Nazis used tiki torches during a rally of extremists in Charlottesville, Virginia, the torches have taken on a new meaning. Now, marching with tiki torches is exclusively the domain of extremists and imbeciles.

I had online debates with the clueless wherein they claimed the torches are "just yard decorations." It's true until you march down the street with them during a protest. If people are really too dense to understand this difference in context, the independence movement is better off without them. Whether one thinks it's fair or not, symbols have meanings that can reflect very badly on an entire movement. Just avoid using controversial symbols at all and don't let others bring them among you. We need to focus on the independence debate itself, not try to explain why tiki torches or Confederate flags appeared in our midst.

The discussion on race, religion, sexual orientation, and so on, certainly has its place. That place, however, isn't in the independence movement. Advocates must keep things simple and focused. When the movement becomes sidetracked into policy debates, particularly social policy, division is sure to follow soon after.

Any encouragement of acts of violence must be dealt with immediately. Never call for the execution of a person or group of people even if you think you are being tongue-in-cheek. Don't put up with it from others. Sharing a depiction of a politician being hanged may seem reasonable to some on the fringe, but what it does is give opponents to independence the opportunity to define the movement as extreme and dangerous.

During the 2021 election campaign, you can be sure Trudeau's strategists were grinning from ear to ear when they saw the video of an idiot throwing "rocks," it was reported, at the prime minister during a campaign appearance. While the pebbles—they were indeed small pebbles—were harmless, the act of pelting missiles crossed a major boundary. Minor violence is still violence. It allowed Team Trudeau to play the victim. Think of it this way, a European soccer player will hurl himself to the ground clutching his shin 'in terrible pain' after a minor foul. The ref will sometimes award a penalty shot for the opposition. The goal scored wins the feigners the match. So, keep this principle in mind: no harm means no foul.

Being needlessly confrontational or aggressive towards the public hurts the cause, too. I was once covering an anti-mask protest and watched some of the protesters blocking traffic in order to call the drivers, who were wearing masks, assholes and communists. How is this supposed to draw supporters to their cause? Nobody tried to constrain these extreme protesters and while there may have been many reasonable and civilized people among the demonstrators, their voices were lost.

The cause is critically important. We have the means to peacefully pursue its goals. There is no need to devolve into violence, or threats of violence. It will only set us back or, worst of all, lead to somebody getting seriously hurt.

Managing this is easier said than done, of course. The person expressing extreme views may be one of the top donors or volunteers within the movement. A person may be one of the kindest and most likeable, yet harbour conspiracy theories about lizard people from outer space. It will be tough to ask these individuals to either keep those views to themselves, or to take their views elsewhere. The stress of having to take a heavy hand with a volunteer or supporter will be much less than that of watching your movement fall apart because someone had one too many beers and decided to express their whacko views at an open microphone, in public.

We need the support from every segment of the population if we want to achieve independence. If ethnic minorities, religious minorities, or members of the LGBTQ+ community feel an independent West won't protect their rights and safety, they won't take part, and who could blame them? As with everything else, we must lead by example. There will always be fringe voices, but we need to make it clear these voices are indeed on the fringe and do not represent the majority.

Don't sweat the small stuff

Movements can devolve into internal strife over the pettiest of issues. I remember observing with frustration as a group of Alberta independence activists spent months fighting over what the post-secession flag would be for a new western nation. The amount of energy wasted was staggering and several supporters stomped out of the virtual room as the debate raged.

Yes indeed, a new nation will need a new flag. To spend time on such branding matters when we still aren't anywhere close to a successful independence vote is a distraction from the real work that needs to be done. There is no need to worry about submitting designs for a presidential palace for the new nation, either. We can deal with those things later.

Part of what motivates people to get embroiled in those issues is they all want to make their own mark on what will presumably be a significant period in history. Folks want to look back and say, "I created that policy" or, "I designed that coat of arms." Wanting to get your contribution on the record is fine, but it can often turn into an obsession with some people. They become single-issue-driven and overly sensitive to critique.

A national constitution will be essential, post-secession. We certainly need some broad discussion and public engagement. Indeed, we can't form a new nation without a new system. If we retain the old system, we are simply creating a smaller version of the nation we just left behind. That said, we must maintain discussion at a high level, certainly at this point. We have to focus on broader concepts of decentralization of power and individual rights, so we must not allow ourselves to become mired in the creation of a new constitution. Let's take one step at a time and keep the appeal of independence broad and stay focused on the goal. Don't be happy to die in the foothills for the cause when we still have the mountain to climb.

Talk it up

Positivity is important even when dealing with a subject that feels negative.

Again, this is an area I find challenging. It's easier to highlight the drawbacks of Confederation than to focus on the positives of independence. We have to sing its praises.

It sounds cliché, but you need to frame independence as a beginning rather than an ending. Independence is an opportunity to create a modern system of government. You can take successful elements of systems from around the world and learn from their mistakes. We *can* have an equitable, democratic, and decentralized system the envy of the planet, if we do it right.

Western independence will be a form of rejuvenation. Frame independence as something we can look forward to rather than being something we feel forced to pursue.

Indeed, the shakeup may make the rest of Canada a better place to live, as well. The remaining provinces will surely be re-examining how they operate and might embrace change for the better.

Take a break

Politics and advocacy can be an exhausting business, mentally, physically, and emotionally. Burnout is bad for both you and the movement. Don't take on more work or responsibility than you can handle, and don't let the inevitable setbacks grind you down.

I've seen some of the most effective political advocates burn out because they couldn't step back. They immersed themselves in a political cause and put everything on the line. Eventually they cracked and quit politics and advocacy completely, and permanently.

Being an ambassador for independence is an important commitment. Invest only the time, money, and energy you can afford, and no more. You will be far more effective if you dedicate a few hours a week over years than if you dive in full-time and flake out after a few months. The line between dedication and obsession can easily be blurred. If you think you're burning out, or if somebody is telling you they think you are heading for the crash zone, take it seriously and take a break. The movement will still be there when you get back.

Western independence will come via the combined efforts of thousands, if not millions of ambassadors for independence. Some will contribute through little more than the occasional conversation or social media post, and some will work at full-steam within parties and groups. The cumulative and decentralized effort of a myriad of individuals is what will bring us to independence. The political parties and groups will come and go, but as long as individuals keep promoting the cause using good judgement, its foundations will continue to strengthen.

We should all be well versed in the case for western independence and able to communicate it effectively to others. Your role as an individual is critical and it's the most important role. Take it seriously and remain discerning and vigilant in your duty.

Chapter 8

HOW TO COUNTER COMMON ARGUMENTS AGAINST INDEPENDENCE

While ongoing battles and arguments are counterproductive, an independence ambassador needs a ready reply for people who are debating the issue. You will repeatedly hear the same old arguments made against independence and it helps to have a practiced counterargument. The person debating you might be intransigent, but someone listening in on the discussion could be receptive to your case. You are always on duty as an ambassador and must be prepared to offer a convincing response to questions.

Don't push it

People have genuine concerns and need their questions answered rationally and politely.

Before getting into the counterpoints to common arguments made against independence, I should begin by introducing one argument that *isn't* worth getting into.

It's inevitable you will encounter those who say, "it's never going to happen!" every time you broach the subject. They will usually repeat the statement in response to any point you try to make. It's easier for them to attempt to shut down the conversation rather than have a rational discussion with you, and they will often increase the volume and tone of their voice as they go on. A person with entrenched views against independence really doesn't want the discussion at all. Your best response is to heed their wishes. Change the subject, leave the room, or start talking to someone else. Nothing you say will sway a person who has an unyielding stance, but you could say a lot to entrench them further in their opposition. You could upset yourself and say things in anger or frustration. This can cast a pall over a dinner party, a lunchroom chat, or wherever you might be engaging a naysayer. It's just not worth it.

It's tough to disengage with someone when you know they're making an unreasonable case, but it's the only potentially productive strategy. Keep in mind people can change their views over time. Perhaps the person claiming independence is impossible is actually only one issue away from becoming receptive to the idea. If you've infuriated them in a fight over the subject, they might never want to discuss it with you—or anyone—again, even if they're beginning to open their mind to it.

Sometimes the best thing to do is close the subject with the old cliché, "Never say never," and move along. They might come around over time, or they might not. Once their heels are digging in, though, there's little sense in expending energy debating further with them.

Landlocked is not hamstrung

A common, shallow argument made against western independence is to claim, "You would be landlocked!" How awful! Why, we could end up just like Switzerland, only with massive reserves of natural resources!

Landlocked nations are nothing new and being landlocked doesn't mean, by any measure, a nation will be poor or dysfunctional. Austria is doing well. Hungary and Slovakia are coming along, too, after having shed the yoke of socialism. Having a coastline doesn't ensure stability or prosperity for a nation. How well have things been working out for Venezuela, or most African nations? Is Bangladesh nearing prosperity and has Vietnam enjoyed a history of peace?

A coastline is certainly an advantage for a nation, but it doesn't guarantee poverty or riches, peace or conflict. The system by which a nation is governed is far more important than its geography.

Let's imagine for a moment Saskatchewan and Alberta both seceded and united as a new nation under a new system. It would be critical to the collective economy that natural resources reach foreign markets and, yes, the new nation would indeed be landlocked. Why, though, is it assumed Eastern Canada, BC, or the US would block the export or import of goods and services?

Secession will surely come with some hard feelings and there will be bumps in the road as new trade agreements are formed, but it's absurd to assume the rest of Canada would be so bitter and self-destructive as to blockade the new nation.

If BC decided to block Alberta and Saskatchewan from getting goods to the coast, the new western nation would of course immediately retaliate by blocking BC's goods from crossing to the East. It would cripple its ports and decimate its economy. Canada's remaining provinces in the East would be in a crunch, too. The impasse wouldn't last long, if indeed it ever happened at all.

European nations have trade disputes all the time, but they don't blockade and starve their neighbours in order to resolve them. It would be too harmful for all involved and modern nations simply don't do that anymore. The US certainly wouldn't want to get into a trade mess by refusing the exchange of goods and services and the flow of people from the new nation. Economic reality trumps hurt feelings. Just look at how Europe continues to buy Russian natural gas while condemning Russia's invasion of Ukraine.

There are international accords established to deal with landlocked nations that could be appealed to at international tribunal, if it ever came to that. Canada itself could face trade sanctions from other nations if it acted unfairly against the new western nation. International trade relies on these agreements being respected and other nations wouldn't support Canada's attempts to starve its new neighbour into submission.

Let's not forget we are *already* landlocked. Canada has allowed Quebec to dictate pipeline access and has been hostile to western efforts to seek alternative markets through eastern coastal access. Our Confederation is already dysfunctional since provincial governments hinder goods from other provinces under present policies. There is no free and open trade of oil—or even beer—in Canada. If anything, a new nation might have more leverage for potential trade agreements with regions than it did while within Confederation.

The case against independence holds no water on the basis the new nation would be landlocked.

The UN: does it matter?

It isn't terribly hard for a nation to gain membership of the UN. Here's the statement on membership requirements from the UN Charter:

> Membership in the United Nations is open to all peace-loving states which accept the obligations

> contained in the present Charter and, in the judgement of the Organization, are able and willing to carry out these obligations.

The UN currently recognizes 193 sovereign member states. How many of those are indeed "peace-loving"?

The UN isn't a terribly exclusive club. The UN would accept a new nation with a constitution and a charter quickly enough, for what it's worth.

An independent west would have no issue becoming part of the UN should it choose to, as well as gaining recognition as a sovereign nation from other countries. Other nations around the world would have little to gain in trying to exclude a new, independent Western Canadian nation from trade and recognition.

The benefits of UN membership are questionable at best, but it wouldn't hurt to take part. And its merits would be debated.

Free movement and mobility

What about international travel, whether between former Canadian provinces or abroad?

There's little reason to believe travel between nations would be tightly restricted after a province or provinces chose independence. Most Canadians have family and friends across the country. While there will doubtless be some hurt feelings the day after a province secedes, no remaining province would cut off access from members of the new nation. Their own citizens would be in uproar and would lead only to more unity challenges.

Provinces already benefit from a migratory workforce moving between them and while there might be a need for a work visa system, it needn't be complicated. We can't assume a province would cut off their own citizens from travel or ban outside visitors. It would devastate tourism and create unjustifiable hardship for families located across Canada. Of course, considering how the Maritime provinces responded to the COVID-19 pandemic, some short-term restrictions aren't out of the realms of possibility. However, if such restrictions were motivated by spite, they wouldn't be sustainable.

A question of numbers

Does the West have a large enough population?

One of the more ridiculous cases made against western independence is we don't have a population large enough to make it on our own.

If a high population count is the recipe for prosperity, political stability, and liberty, why isn't India leading the world on all those fronts? How about China or Russia? They all have large populations, but is it necessarily an advantage? Many of the most stable and prosperous countries on earth with the highest standards of living have a population of ten million, or fewer. Sweden, Austria, and New Zealand are doing well with small populations.

There are also some less populous nations in poverty and misery, of course. The population of a nation is not the prime factor determining the viability or success of a nation. The management of the nation is what counts.

Drawing the lines of governance

What's to keep cities or other regions from partitioning? If secession were to happen on the basis of Canada's legislation, only provinces could secede. It's not an ability granted to other levels of government.

There could very possibly be some jurisdictions where there'd be no majority support for independence, though I wouldn't anticipate too many pockets holding out if we faced a situation where the majority of a province had chosen to secede.

Regarding post-independence partitioning, would the new nation assume the same, centralized system of governance they had just seceded from? It's pretty doubtful.

I use the Swiss system as an example of a new system in a later chapter. Switzerland is a fraction the size of any Canadian province, it has four official languages, it's divided into twenty-six relatively independent governing units, and it's one of the most unified nations in the world. With a decentralized system of governance, regional differences can be accounted for and respected.

Unity will be achieved through decentralized power. When smaller regions and populations have respect and local autonomy, they don't pursue independence. A new state won't have the broken system Canada currently has.

In defense of the nation

Opponents of independence like to point to the military as if it would present some intractable problem upon secession. While there will certainly be complications in dealing with the armed forces, it won't be impossible to resolve. Independence doesn't happen overnight after a yes vote. It is going to take time and negotiation, and the disposition of the military will be an important part of that transition.

Military assets will need to be divided—people, equipment, and intelligence. Many westerners are serving on eastern military bases while western bases have many easterners. No one should be prevented from migrating to whichever part of the new nation or the former nation they choose once partition occurs. This will leave some gaps since specialized personnel aren't easily replaced, particularly in a small military. Consideration for military personnel and their families is essential.

People claim an independent West couldn't afford its own military and only in union with Canada can we bear the cost. They obviously don't understand fiscal deficit in Canada and the broader economic picture. Ottawa takes more from the West in taxes than it returns in services, and this includes the military. We could afford a scaled-down military force proportional to our population and still have surplus cash when compared to our current bill for Canadian Forces.

Opponents often ask, "Without Canada's military, what would keep foreign nations from marching in and taking over the West?"

This case against independence is ludicrous. Do we really believe for a second Canada's military is what keeps China, Russia, or even the US from invading us?

While there are fantastic, brave people serving in Canada's armed forces, let's not pretend the Canadian forces are of a size or strength to stop any significant invasion for more than a few minutes. Our southern neighbour's military might be what truly protects us and that won't change in the event of independence. Not that the US is obligated to defend Canada, but they certainly wouldn't tolerate the arrival of military forces from an expansionist nation at their border and the occupation their northern ally and neighbour—it just isn't in the cards.

The size, scope, and nature of a military force in an independent west are up for discussion. Would there be a peacekeeping role? Would it just be a mandate to defend? Would the force simply specialize in domestic issues such as natural disasters? These are all important questions, but they are all topics that merit discussion after a positive vote on secession, not before. There are simply too many variables to debate at this point and to do so now would lead to division within the independence movement.

It goes without saying an independent west will be entitled to its share of existing military assets.

To honour the fallen

Opponents of independence will often pull the emotional card: "Our forefathers fought for Canada!"

No. Our forefathers fought and made the ultimate sacrifice for *freedom*, it just happened to be under the Canadian flag. The principles for which they fought extend far beyond the boundaries of any nation's singular identity. Nations change, the need for freedom does not.

We should and will still honour the sacrifices made by those before us for the freedoms we enjoy today. Western independence doesn't erase history, it just opens a new chapter.

It would actually be an insult to those who fought wars on our behalf if we allowed our freedoms to continue to be eroded. We are fortunate in that we can fight at the ballot box rather than on the battlefield, and we will never forget those who fought for our freedom to do so.

Our forefathers certainly didn't fight and die so Justin Trudeau can invoke martial law upon peacefully protesting citizens, or fire off his unilateral diktats from Ottawa via orders-in-council.

How will we preserve those freedoms and civil rights gained through the sacrifices of our forefathers? We cannot do so if we don't emerge successfully from the unsatisfactory status quo. We can honour and preserve those freedoms under a new nation where they can be constitutionally enshrined, protected, and respected.

New nations and First Nations

Folks often assert secession is impossible because indigenous groups won't participate. There are two problems with this contention. Firstly, they make the assumption indigenous people are satisfied with how Confederation has been working for them. The other hole in the argument is despite labelling indigenous reserves as "nations," there is no legal nation-to-nation negotiation required. Indigenous reserves are a construct of the federal government. We don't need full consensus from First Nations to achieve independence.

Let's face it. The reserve system is an utter catastrophe and most people trapped on reserves are living in misery. By every measure, government policies regarding First Nations in Canada have been an abject failure and there are no indications anything will improve under the current system. Life expectancy, education, health, wealth, and safety are all at disgracefully low levels on the reserves. How bad will we let it get before we do something meaningful about it? How many more generations will be born into a system of dependency and despair?

What western independence can offer is a way to help First Nations break free from this broken paradigm. Western independence doesn't represent a threat to indigenous people, it actually presents an opportunity. They will never prosper within Canada under the Indian Act and the apartheid reserve system it serves. We can't tinker with and repair it, it's rotten to the core and needs to be torn down. Western independence could liberate indigenous people from this system of self-serving bureaucrats.

But what of the treaties?

I've read the treaties, unlike many who present themselves as advocates for indigenous peoples. The original treaties were pretty simple documents. Most of the content of a typical treaty is the definition of the boundaries of reserve lands. They include details about funding entitlement for chiefs and councillors and some obligations for provisions such as farm implements. Paradoxically, there was usually a commitment to educate the children on the reserve—the basis for residential schools was a treaty right. If nothing else, this should serve to remind us just how outdated treaties are and how exploitative and oppressive governments can be. It's absurd to try to stick to the letter of those antiquated agreements.

The treaties also made no bones about the permanent ceding of all other lands outside the defined reserves. It was made as clear as day the indigenous signatories were giving up all claims to lands outside of their reserves, forever.

Treaties and their modern interpretations are a mess. Advocates demand we must honour those documents then become very selective about which parts we honour. Activist judges have reinterpreted the treaties in an attempt see ancient agreements through a modern lens. It appears not to have improved our indigenous peoples' lot in life in any measurable way.

Most laws governing First Nations are packed into the Indian Act and are not defined by the treaties. The Indian Act is a vile, racist document and it has done immeasurable damage to indigenous people and their relationships with non-indigenous people. If we are to talk about true systemic racism, the Indian Act is the very definition of it. Many lawyers, bureaucrats and politicians prosper greatly by the Indian Act, and they fight any attempt to modify or abolish it. One benefit of western independence would be the abolition of the entrenched, race-based policies that have so poorly served indigenous people.

The land boundaries defined in the treaties can and should be respected. In an independent west with a heavily decentralized system of governance, indigenous reserves can be transitioned into independent governance units such as the Swiss cantons I describe in another chapter. Indigenous people will no longer be locked within those dead-end, racial enclaves we call reserves. They will have land, legislation, and the ability to participate in the economy on the exact same standing as anyone else. They would have the opportunity to prosper or fail like any other citizen. Many ambitious indigenous people have been thwarted in their attempts to form businesses or become personally independent because the reserve system holds them back.

It won't be simple or easy. Anyone who thinks there's a fine future for indigenous people within the current model in Canada clearly hasn't studied or spent time on indigenous reserves. They are hopeless dependencies that can't be fixed. They were created on an abhorrently racist and primitive model. Independence provides the means to break people out of the current cycle of abuse and thereafter prosper without the sacrifice of culture and identity.

There is no form of legislative veto on the part of First Nations in Canada. We don't need 100 percent consensus on the part of indigenous people to become independent, nor will we ever get it. We must argue the case that independence will benefit indigenous people and we need to approach them with respect and humility. They are the most established of western peoples and have been the most roughly treated by Confederation.

SOS

What about emergencies? Could an independent west deal with events such as natural disasters?

It's nice to know you have neighbours who will watch your back if you get into trouble. Why would we assume such neighbourly goodwill wouldn't exist post-independence? Alberta sent firefighters as far as Australia when they had their devastating wildfires, and Mexico sent firefighters to BC. For the most part, the world is a caring place, and we will look out for each other even when international borders stretch between us.

In the event of a natural disaster, we can be confident an independent west would act to lend aid to Canada without hesitation and that Canada would reciprocate. Those who feel Canada would withhold aid to neighbouring nations in times of crisis apparently hold Canada in low esteem. It's a petty and wrongheaded attitude. Remember, our issue is with the system, not the people. Canadians are generous souls living within a broken system. They will remain the same generous and compassionate people when a new system arises.

Economic mojo

Is the West's economy diverse enough? Opponents to western independence often will cry, "You don't have the economic diversity to survive on your own!"

Tell that to Qatar where a small population enjoys the highest per-capita income in the world despite being an almost purely oil-driven economy.

Western Canada's economy is predominantly natural resource driven. When world demand for lumber, petrochemicals, potash, and food is constantly increasing, we are not poorly placed to prosper in providing those resources. How could we have expanded beyond our agrarian economy a century ago when forced to pay central Canadian manufacturers a premium for farm implements? And, while also being forced to sell product to them at a discount?

Western Canada has been drained to prop up Central Canada's manufacturing sector since the beginning of Confederation. Now the manufacturing sector is a shadow of what it once was, Central Canada simply spreads our money out via transfer payments for social programs.

The economy of the West is far more diverse than people give it credit for. In Alberta for example, while oil, gas, and mining are indeed very lucrative, they make up less than 17 percent of Alberta's GDP. Light manufacturing, tech services, and financial services have been fast-growing sectors in the West for quite some time. Manitoba and Saskatchewan have much more to offer than just their agricultural sectors, and BC already has a very diverse economy.

Western Canada still has enough petrochemical resources in reserve for an entire generation to prosper. It's well understood that world demand for petrochemical products will be increasing for decades despite the best efforts of ideologically driven politicians to switch the world to inefficient and expensive renewable energy sources. Our oil and gas resources won't last forever, but they will be profitable for quite some time. Rather than shutting in our resources in anticipation of a world transition that won't come for a while, we should be increasing our extraction of those resources. If demand for a resource is finite, it only makes sense to make the most of it while we can. The wealth attained through resource extraction can be used to diversify and plan the economy for the next generation.

Economic diversity doesn't come through government subsidies. That's a mistake governments on all levels continue to make in their efforts to promote it. Demand—not donation—is what dictates diversification. Industries reliant on subsidies either become perpetual parasites or fail as soon as the subsidies end. Using wealth gained through resource extraction to diversify the economy doesn't mean pouring the resource revenue into other industries. The prosperity secured from non-renewable resources can be used to get government out of the way and create a positive business environment.

Proponents of coerced economic diversification often view things in a binary way. They think shutting down conventional energy production is the only way to develop alternative means of production. We need only look to Germany and their energy crisis to see how short-sighted and dangerous such an approach is.

In the late 1980s, the Alberta government tried to diversify the economy through investments in new businesses and it was a catastrophe. Companies such as MagCan, Novatel and the Swan Hills plant bled taxpayers for hundreds of millions of dollars and went broke within years of being formed. Governments can't pick winners, but losers can pick governments. Subsidy whores and effective lobbyists robbed taxpayers of billions over the decades and contributed nothing towards economic diversity.

In the 1990s, Alberta embraced the Alberta Advantage strategy under premier Ralph Klein. Klein dramatically shrank government while reducing taxes and regulations. Alberta was declared open for business and it worked. Head offices began relocating to Alberta to take advantage of lower taxes while new creative enterprises formed and flourished. Economic diversification doesn't need to be complicated. Government just needs to get out of the way.

The prime impediment to western economic diversification is Central Canada. Since entering confederation in 1905, Alberta alone has been drained of over $600 billion in net contributions to Canada through taxes taken for services never delivered. How can a province create a business-friendly environment with competitive taxation when surplus dollars are syphoned off and poured into competing eastern companies such as Bombardier? They can't.

Central Canadian interference in the western economy has turned us into an investment pariah. With energy projects being shut down or regulated into bankruptcy by the federal government, the West has been economically hamstrung. Who in their right mind would invest in a region that has a hostile federal government with a propensity to attack its industries?

The shutdown of pipeline expansions to both coasts coupled with a ban on tanker traffic on the West Coast has left the West with only the United States as a prime customer. Consequently, western energy products are sold at a heavy discount when compared with world prices. That bleeds the western economy and keeps taxes high and discourages investment in all local industries and initiatives, not just oil and gas.

With foreign investment being chased away and with our profits being drained, we simply can't afford to create the business environment required for economic diversification. Central Canada prefers us as a natural resource-dependent colony and they work actively to keep us that way. We'll never break out of the roller-coaster economics of dependency on world resource prices until we break out of the system that keeps us there.

The West is already economically diverse and will become more so upon independence. The diversity argument against the pursuit of independence has no merit. Western Canada has an abundance of natural resources. The revenue from those resources will enable us to create one of the most welcoming business environments in the world. We have a skilled, educated, and resourceful population. We all can and will live in prosperity once independent from Canada.

A question of debt

What about the national debt?

This is a more complicated issue. Canada's national debt is colossal and it's growing. It's one of the important reasons the West should extricate itself from this pending fiscal catastrophe. All provinces are guilty of deficit financing in recent times.

Since the 1960s, Alberta alone has contributed over $622 billion to Confederation without services in return. Alberta makes up about 12 percent of Canada's population. If anything, Alberta should get a refund on leaving Confederation. BC has traditionally been a net contributor and Saskatchewan has—for some time now—been pouring more money into Canada than it gets in return. Manitoba has always been a net recipient of transfers of funds within Canada.

A reckoning of Canada's capital assets would have to happen—federal buildings, military bases, and so on. This again would work in favour of the West since federal expenditures have been disproportionately funnelled into Eastern Canada for generations. How many hundreds of millions of dollars went to the Canadian Firearms Centre in New Brunswick for the failed firearms registry of the 1990s for example? On the division of assets, we in the West can rest assured we wouldn't owe anything to the rest of Canada.

It's going to take some time and negotiation, and while the Clarity Act demands the federal government negotiates in good faith, we can't count on that. The West should be acting to extricate itself from its fiscal ties with Canada sooner rather than later. We need to form our own pension plans, police forces, and tax collection systems just as Quebec already has.

The bottom line is this: Canada owes the West more than the West owes Canada. Canada could claim the West somehow owes it money, but how could they collect? Even if we negotiated to take some or all of the national debt pro rata based per capita on our population, we would still be no worse off than we are today. We really have nothing to lose in that regard.

How would being invested in massive federal debt be a good reason to stay within Confederation? It really isn't one of the stronger cases made against independence, yet federalists try to make it.

Show me the money

When it comes to a new currency, the world is our oyster.

There are 180 currencies in the world right now. Adding a new one won't be terribly difficult. In the digital age, printing and coinage are required but aren't a priority.

It's easy enough for a new nation to issue its own currency. The biggest battles will be over whose effigies grace the coins and notes and what to name the currency.

What about private assets owned in multiple provinces?

Numerous companies have assets distributed across various provinces along with their employees who travel between them. A good number of citizens also own property outside their home province. We cannot seize property from people and businesses simply because they're not resident here. Neither can we block ready access to those assets. Such a move would be immoral and would be economically catastrophic.

Many close nations have relatively permissive rules between one another when it comes to foreign property ownership and access. There already exist models we could follow. Sweden and Norway come to mind—they don't require passports for travel between their nations. We shouldn't assume an impenetrable border would suddenly appear in the event of a positive vote for independence.

Different corporate tax structures between provinces are also nothing new and companies are adaptable.

It will be beneficial for all jurisdictions to keep access as open as possible for people whether that's regarding employment, business, or access to assets.

People jump to the very misguided conclusion that an independent region would cut off all access to other provinces out of sheer spite. While that isn't impossible, it's highly unlikely. The damage done to both economic jurisdictions would simply be too much. Everyone will benefit from rational negotiation and there is little reason to believe this can't or won't happen.

There should be few obstacles in the way for companies or people who want to liquidate their assets, post-independence. Not every investor will want to be a part of the new nation. They should be allowed to relocate without penalty. An independent west needs to remain consistently supportive of enterprise, even if it is leaving the

Confederation. A dedication to trustworthy business dealings will reduce investment chill caused by the dissolution of the federation.

Culture and identity

Can the West go independent without a distinct culture? Independence opponents like to claim the West has no culture. What the West has is a diverse culture. Unlike Quebec where, for example, the French language provides a clear cultural identity, western culture's characteristics are more subtle.

One of my more embarrassing moments while leading the Alberta Independence Party was when a media member asked me to define western culture. I had just referenced the term in a speech at a town hall meeting and when asked about it, I didn't have a good or ready answer. The next day, a mocking article was published in the *Globe and Mail* about how the leader of a western independence party couldn't even define western culture. It was a fair question on the part of the reporter, and I ought to have had a ready answer.

While there's no concise answer to the question of western Canadian culture, we most definitely have culture. It says a great deal about Central Canada's attitude in that they tend to imply the West has no distinguishable culture. Would they dare suggest Quebec doesn't have a distinct culture? Of course not.

Travelling across Canada, one can't help but sense the cultural differences even if it's difficult to describe them. No one can deny Newfoundland and Labrador have a unique culture, and it goes far beyond a linguistic accent. Cultural differences between neighbouring Maritime provinces are more subtle but are still distinct. Southern Ontario has a very different disposition than Northern Ontario, and Canada's lower mainland on the West Coast is a world all its own. Why is it considered laughable to claim the western prairie region has a distinct culture, much less one worth preserving?

Federalists don't want to acknowledge cultural distinctions among regions that might be considering secession. They will always attempt to define Canada as one big happy culturally homogeneous family.

The Greater Toronto Area has a distinct culture, too, and it can be described as a self-centred form of vanity. Canadians joke that Torontonians don't realize anything exists beyond what they can see from the top of the CN Tower. They are an introverted lot and no one would accuse them of thinking poorly of Western Canada. The thing is, they don't think much about Western Canada at all—we might as well be our own country already. At best they see us as distant cousins who are an ignoble version of *them*. We certainly don't merit the status of a region that has its own distinct culture.

Western Canadian culture doesn't have easily distinguishable attributes such as language or race. We do maintain something of a rugged individualism, however. We want the freedom to take care of ourselves and to take care of our neighbours without the government always getting in the way. There's pride in self-determination, and ambition is applauded. We aren't asking to be taken care of, we just want to be left alone. That's not to say we won't continue to care about others, we simply want to ensure our charity is direct and on our own terms. We value a tight local community more than we value our place in a broader federal one.

This attitude stems from our region being more recently settled, relatively speaking. Immigrants to the West—whether at the end of the 1800s or in the last ten years—have usually moved this way seeking opportunity. They've often come from countries where the state itself was the biggest hindrance to their ambitions and they have little appetite for intrusive government. Westerners chafe under local government as it is, they sure as hell don't want to abide by the dictates of a distant central government.

I don't think it's as much a Western Canada thing as it is a western North American thing. After the oil price crash of 2008, I spent a lot of time working on projects throughout the United States. I never quite felt comfortable working in New York, Pennsylvania, and West Virginia. I'm not knocking the people, I just didn't fit in.

I loved working in Texas, Wyoming, and Oklahoma, however. The people that way shared the same sense of ambition and individualism as we do. I encountered initiative among people rather than a sense of entitlement. They maintained neighbourly courtesy and, of course, the same distaste for central government. Western Canada has more in common with Texans, culturally speaking, than they do with southern Ontarians. I am not saying that as if it's a bad thing, many people in Central Canada would see it the same way.

During my time moving in Canadian political circles, I've had opportunity to interact with some very wealthy folks. Alas, although I only have modest resources myself, I did get to attend many conferences and speak with some affluent people. You really notice the differences between wealthy Easterners and the well-heeled folks from the West.

Western money is often new and, yes, usually the result of energy sector success and of those people who've spent time working hard in the field. Eastern money tends to be old money, not that every wealthy Easterner was born into their money, but most of them were. They make up part of the Laurentian Elite we so often hear about.

You really get to see the difference between a champagne socialist and a self-made person when you interact with folks from both sides of that divide. The former is loaded with entitlement while the latter full of optimism. The powerbrokers in the East and West both reflect their respective populations and are distinctly different. If we can't call those differences cultural, then what are they?

Perhaps I fail to define western culture in a nutshell, but it is this: distinct, real, and something better experienced than defined. We enjoy a unique, healthy, and vibrant culture, even if it's tough to put your finger on it. We can't let opponents to independence claim it's non-existent, not for a second.

Same shit, different day

Don't we just need to change the party in power in Ottawa?

Support for western independence ebbs and flows. We see spikes in support of independence when hostile Liberal governments are in power in Ottawa, while support for independence wanes when less hostile Conservative governments are in power. Both parties tend to screw the West in the end, it's just that the federal Conservatives sometimes feel a little remorse when they do it. It doesn't matter which federal party has the reins in Ottawa, if a party wants to get in and stay in power, they need to pander to Central Canada, and it's always at the expense of the West. It's not even malicious, really, it's just a reality borne of our broken system of Confederation.

In the last few decades, what have federal Conservative parties in power actually achieved to curb alienation of the West?

While former Conservative prime minister Brian Mulroney wooed the West in the early 1980s with the promise of ending Pierre Trudeau's National Energy Program, he waited two and a half years after his election before he did it. By then, world oil prices had collapsed and, ironically, Alberta would have benefited from the program had he done it sooner. Mulroney then screwed Manitoba by awarding a billion-dollar maintenance contract for CF-18 fighter jets to Quebec's Canadair rather than Bristol Aerospace of Winnipeg, this despite Bristol's bid being obviously superior to Canadair's. Mulroney was unapologetic for his vote pandering to Quebec while Liberal and NDP opposition members also refused to stand up for Manitoba in any meaningful way. Every party leader was well aware they couldn't afford to alienate Quebec on the issue from a political standpoint, so they hung Manitoba out to dry. Liberal, Tory, same old story.

Those kinds of behaviours led to the decimation of the Progressive Conservative Party of Canada in the West when the Reform Party was created. That in turn led to over a decade of Liberal control of the federal government where former prime minister Jean Chrétien made no bones about his indifference to the needs of the West. In the 2000 federal election, Chrétien only appeared in Alberta twice in almost forty days of campaigning and both times was only briefly in Edmonton. He barely made his presence known in the rest of the West. For this, Chrétien's Liberals were rewarded with a strong majority government.

When Conservatives were finally united enough to win another majority under Stephen Harper in 2011, how much did Harper do for the West? There's no doubt Stephen Harper was friendly to Western Canada, which was refreshing to say the least, but what did he change?

As a Calgarian prime minister with a majority government in Ottawa, Stephen Harper didn't manage to make any lasting changes to government in favour of the West. Despite being one of the prime authors and proponents of the Alberta Agenda, Harper didn't promote any of the tenets of that letter while serving as prime minister. Furthermore, while holding a solid majority government, Harper didn't amend the equalization formula that continued to bleed the western coffers to subsidize Quebec. While Harper did appoint a few elected senators, he didn't make any real efforts to pursue Senate reform.

It wasn't that Stephen Harper was an odious traitor to the West, it's only that Harper was smart enough to understand the path to the prime minister's seat never runs through the West. If Harper had stuck to his old Reform Party roots, he would simply have been another in a string of Conservative opposition leaders. Harper instead became pragmatic, served Central Canada, and managed to get a single term as PM with a majority. I can't help but wonder if Harper knew he would never get a second majority had he tried to bring in some real reforms during his single term. We will never know.

It's not prejudice that forces federal leaders to serve Central Canada at the expense of the rest of the country, it's a question of math. It is impossible to win a majority government in Canada without winning a large portion of seats in Quebec and Ontario. Canada's appointed Senate is little more than a joke and does nothing to stand up for regional inequities despite being ostensibly created to do so. The Canadian system is like a large funnel that pours resources from the outer regions into the centre. Any efforts by a federal party to buck that system will lead to an electoral loss.

There's little sense getting upset with federal parties that turn their backs on the West. We need to recognize the futility of effecting any real change through them. Federal Conservative governments don't do us any more favours than Liberal ones. We should just vote for regionally based federal parties as we did with the original Reform Party and then dedicate our best efforts towards local political organization in the pursuit of independence. Pouring time, resources, and emotional energy into federal parties in the hope of making real change is wasteful and heartbreaking. Backing off on the pursuit of independence during periods of federal Conservative government is counterproductive—not that we need to worry about seeing a federal Conservative government any time soon.

Ask any federal Conservative leader what they will do with the Soviet-style supply management system in Canada that robs consumers in order to fund Quebec dairy cartels, for example. They won't dare oppose that rotten policy for a second, even though it goes against every conservative principle in the book. The system will beat a political party every time.

In his final days as Alberta's premier in 2022, Jason Kenney repeatedly claimed any moves towards independence would create capital flight from Alberta. It was disingenuous partisan play. Kenney was vindictive and bitter about the support Danielle Smith had gathered in the race to replace him as the leader of the United Conservative Party and he resorted to fearmongering in an attempt to garner support for his own preferred successor. Unfortunately, such fearmongering can be damaging to the independence cause.

The case made against independence alleging that instability drives away investment reminds me of opponents' assertions that being landlocked is also an argument against it. Confederation is already driving investment away from the West. Independence movements couldn't scare investment away nearly as effectively as a hostile federal government has already done.

For years, major capital investment projects in the West have been regulated out of existence, or outright shut down by an ideologically driven government. There was hardly a peep from Ottawa when US President Biden killed the Keystone XL pipeline project with an executive order within days of taking office in 2021. And Ottawa is deafeningly silent while Quebec shuts down the possibility of a pipeline to the East Coast.

Meanwhile, the West is bearing the fiscal burden so central Canadians can be subsidized.

It's already tough to bring capital investment into the West when investors fear being shut down by the federal government. Independence wouldn't make that any worse and very likely would result in the West's economic landscape becoming far more attractive.

Chapter 9

POLITICAL PARTIES AND HOW TO PARTICIPATE IN THEM

To most people, political parties are mysterious animals. We hear of them and understand how they impact us, but most of us don't take part or understand exactly how they function. If more people don't become directly involved in party organizations, those parties will be subject to the whims of a tiny minority.

People are often frustrated with the indifference displayed by politicians between elections. When they are seeking your vote, it seems you can't escape them; they're phoning, knocking on your door, and filling your mailbox on a daily basis. After the election, most of them vanish. If you want to influence these people *between* elections, you need work within the party.

Let's begin by saying we can't keep trying to change things in those parties that have independence as a main platform. I know, that sounds odd in a book that purports to promote western independence. I'm not trying to tell independence supporters to go underground or give up on party politics. I am using my experience and a pragmatic approach to point out a hard reality. Bear with me.

One-trick pony

Political parties are an intrinsic part of our system and no push for independence will be successful without their involvement. While party members and even elected representatives can be openly in support of western independence, no party should explicitly promote independence objectives as part of their mandate or identity. It leads to division, dilution of the vote, and will set back the independence movement. If anything, the constant spawning of political parties for independence divides the movement when people should be working as one for the common goal. People only have so much capital in dollars, time, and emotion to invest in political movements. If their resources are split too many ways, the secession movement will atrophy.

Advocates for independence should be involved in political parties. It's only through direct party involvement we can be assured pro-independence candidates are selected in nominations and that policies always reflect the interests of the West. That said, a party that goes by independence in name, or as its primary mandate will soon be dead in the water.

The first problem with an explicitly secessionist party is that it turns it into a single-issue entity. The party might have all the best possible policies—it won't matter. As soon as secession is in the name, it's the brand identity people will focus on and it will dilute support immediately. No one is going to ask a candidate with the Marijuana Party what their stance is on public health care is, neither will anyone concern themselves with the education policies of the Green Party. This is what keeps these parties in the realm of protest- and fringe-voter options. They certainly can get messaging out on their prime issues, but they have limited impact on electoral outcomes because of their one-dimensional nature.

I understand the impatience only too well, and the desire to take something of a purist, partisan approach to western independence. When I founded the Alberta Independence Party in 2000, I had the party pursue nothing less than full independence. At our founding convention, a motion was put forward to embrace the term "Separation if necessary, but not necessarily separation." I was angry and frustrated. I believed we'd immediately sacrificed our entire reason for being simply for the sake of political expediency. I was right and wrong at the same time.

I respected the will of the membership, however, and heading into the election, I abided by the policy of soft-separatist campaign messaging. While our candidates did relatively well as far as independent candidates go, none came anywhere close to impacting a local race. Mine was the constituency of Banff-Cochrane and I received a paltry 4 percent of the vote while our best candidate got 8 percent. I felt at the time our poor electoral showing was due to our flaccid stance on independence. We offered little distinction from other conservative entities in the field.

When the 2004 Alberta provincial election came, there was a registered independence party in the mix. The Separation Party of Alberta (SPA) entered the election with twelve candidates. Surely, a registered political party with no ambiguity about its secession goals would do much better than it did in 2001 right? Wrong.

On average, SPA candidates received about 3 percent of the vote in their constituency. I received 2.9 percent of the vote in Highwood. It was an electoral blowout. The SPA failed to make any significant inroads and went pretty much unnoticed during the election. We learned some hard lessons, one especially: an explicitly secessionist party can't gain traction on the electoral road.

While I was door knocking during the campaign, I couldn't escape the reality that we were a single-issue party. The only thing we talked about was secession. How could we speak on issues such as taxation, health care, pensions, and so on? People couldn't know if we offered any benefit.

We also learned just how divisive and noxious the word "separatist" is. Violent separatist movements around the world have created for it very negative connotations. While the intent was to avoid ambiguity, the separatist reference in our party's name made us unsaleable. Now, I use the term "independence" or "secession." I recommend others do the same.

Delegate the cause

While individuals will be the core of the movement, they still need to organize together eventually. Advocacy groups—rather than political parties—should be the prime drivers when it comes to promoting the independence movement. When the time comes for a referendum on independence, we will need strong, grassroots organization. The basic principles of electioneering will still apply during a referendum period: door knocking, literature drops, voter identification, and getting supporters out to vote. An advocacy group can do all those things while keeping their eye on the prize. Gone is the challenge of managing scores of candidates while trying to sell a weighty and nuanced policy set, gone is the quagmire of nominations and conflict over policy making. The goal will be to achieve a yes vote in the referendum, and nothing else. A political party can't maintain such a narrow focus in any campaign, whether in a referendum or general election.

Also, advocacy groups will have an important role to play in the lead-up to a referendum. It will take a lot of public education to bring about the necessary conditions for a yes vote. Town hall meetings and rallies should be held. Studies, polls, and discussion papers need to be released. Counterarguments need to be ready—opponents *will* challenge the independence movement. Groups can present speakers who will stick with the messaging of independence rather than having to deal with the myriad of issues politicians face.

We can and must have several advocacy groups. There are different roles each can specialize in. Some might take on think-tank roles while others will organize public events. Some will lobby elected officials while others work the ground door knocking and training volunteers for when the time comes for a referendum. While there's always a degree of competition between advocacy groups, it isn't nearly as tribal as it is with political parties. People can and often participate in more than one group. We see it with the number of energy advocacy groups in the West, for example.

Having different advocacy groups promoting independence keeps us from putting all our eggs in one basket. Political parties and advocacy groups come and go and are often quite explosive on the way out. Unfortunately, poor leadership, infighting, or even corruption happens.

A group can go from being credible to being a shambles, virtually overnight. Having different advocacy groups also makes it tougher for opponents to destabilize the movement. Decentralized movements are tough to disperse, while single entities are very vulnerable.

Independence groups aren't as constrained by provincial borders as parties are. Opinion polls have consistently shown people are much more receptive to the idea of independence when western provinces work in unison rather than fight alone. While each province will ultimately have to hold their own referendum, it doesn't mean advocates must all stay within their respective provinces. Across the West, advocacy groups can collaborate and share resources in ways political parties cannot.

Don't spectate—activate and participate

If independence groups do their jobs effectively, more people will embrace independence and politicians will follow. Nothing inspires a politician more than the need to preserve their job. If independence advocates successfully promote the idea of secession in a constituency, politicians will embrace the cause. While many politicians are leaders, most are followers. They put their finger to the wind and position themselves to take advantage of prevailing public sentiment.

Elected officials and political parties will remain critically important to the independence movement. It will be impossible to invoke a referendum without the party in power having already provided compelling citizen-inspired legislation. Independence supporters should get into the belly of the partisan political beast, nominate independence-minded candidates, and ensure the necessary policies to facilitate independence are implemented. Having a party in power—or in opposition—sympathetic to the cause will be of paramount importance as we move towards western independence. If a party holds independence as its raison d'être, it will not win government power or even opposition status. We need to leave that secession identity to the advocacy groups.

While political parties with a full secessionist mandate are destined to fail, political parties still remain essential to the independence movement. We will never get the citizen-led referendum legislation we need or create the conditions required to win an independence referendum without a large amount of partisan work. We need to actively participate within political parties if we want the independence agenda to move forward and we need to encourage other independence-minded people to do the same.

Politicians will happily pay lip service to independence advocates in the run-up to an election. They often forget about their regional allegiances, however, once they win a seat in the legislature or Parliament. When they're seeking our vote—or donations—politicians can appear unavoidable. Between elections, though, they can be as rare as hens' teeth.

The best way to stay in touch with and influence politicians is to be active *in* the party.

While Canada's had a partisan political system since the beginning of Confederation, our participation rate is appallingly low. On average, only 2 percent of Canadians are members of a political party. Political parties impact every aspect of our lives yet only one in fifty of us bother even to buy membership. Is it really any surprise when political leadership can be so offside on public opinion?

Dismal public participation in political parties can be an advantage for the independence movement if we capitalize on it. While current support for western independence might not be in majority numbers among the general population, there are enough independence supporters to dominate the membership of some political parties. Think about how unions dominate policymaking in progressive parties despite the fact that most members of the general population are not union members. Unions know how to organize and target activities within parties, and it works.

While the actions of political parties impact every facet of our lives, we don't regard participation important or worthy. We aren't taught the workings of parties in school or how to get involved. People shy away from participation because they simply don't know what's involved. The tribal nature of party politics can put people off, too.

Active party membership is easy and, believe it or not, can actually be fun and satisfying. The degree of involvement is up to the individual. You can simply hold a membership to stay up to date on things, or you can work your way up to election candidate nomination. You can serve on committees and help with elections. You will have an influence on the direction of the party, even between elections.

Parties have a few levels of organization. The offices of the leader, the caucus, and the party organization are three separate but connected entities. While they all form part of the same organization, they all have different responsibilities, and they don't always agree with one another.

Most people only see the outward actions of leaders and elected officials. Party business remains in the background. The party is where the leader and elected officials are selected and official policy is created.

So, where to begin?

Choose your party.

A cynical refrain one often hears with regards to politicians and parties is, "They're all the same!"

Once you start shopping for party membership, you'll discover pretty quickly the parties are in fact all quite different. The decision about which party to join isn't to be taken lightly. You might be investing a great deal of time, emotion, and energy in the months and years ahead. It would all go to waste on a party you might end up abandoning. In other words, treat it like any other relationship—choose carefully.

There are benefits to involvement in a large, mainstream party and there are also benefits to be had with smaller ones. Both have influence. In every province the party in power must eventually comprise enough independence supporters to bring real, workable, citizen-led referendum legislation into being.

In some relationships, the expression "size doesn't matter" gets bandied about. I'm not sure how true that is in the romantic world but there is certainly some truth in it when it comes to political parties. While the biggest parties clearly pack the most punch, don't underestimate the influence a smaller party can have.

Elected officials are always shoulder checking for up-and-comers. If officials want to keep their jobs, they must make strategic decisions. If a nascent party is pulling support from an incumbent politician, that politician will often pivot their actions to deflate support for the competing party and its candidate, especially if the politician is in a swing riding and won their seat on a small margin.

It's frustrating having policies and ideas co-opted when you're part of a small party, but if achieving change is the goal, does it matter who sings the anthem?

Small parties are more flexible and you can have a more tangible impact on the policies and direction of a party, if you so choose. For those with ambition, it can be easier to communicate directly with the party leadership and to move up the ranks.

Small parties have disadvantages, too, of course. They can be vulnerable to hijacking by extremist groups, they have limited resources and they have a hell of a time grabbing the media and public's attention. It takes years—or sometimes decades—for a small party to get established within the political landscape.

When you're choosing a party to join, choose one that best matches your outlook and goals. It's far more important than a party's size. While the Alberta NDP is ahead in support and fundraising (at the time of writing), it would be foolish for an independence-minded person to join them since the NDP has no time for the independence debate. Socialism calls for centralized governance rather than regional autonomy. On the other hand, while the marginal Wildrose Independence Party in Alberta is the truest to indcpendence, it's an organizational basket case and energy spent there could be wasted.

Researching political parties is easier than ever. Every registered political party is listed on the website of the local electoral authority. Any party with more than a dozen members will have a social media presence and their policies will be on a website somewhere. It shouldn't take long to find a party, or three, worthy of joining.

Yes, I said "or three." There's nothing stopping you from taking out a membership with more than one party, personal budget allowing. Membership in most parties costs between $5 and $15 per year. The federal Liberal party offers free membership (you get what you pay for). Some parties will have a clause within their constitution banning members from holding memberships with other parties, but that rule is unenforceable. Parties would have to share their membership lists with each other and that's never likely to happen. If you have the time and energy and believe you can help promote independence within more than one party, go for it.

I bought a membership. Now what?

The first thing you'll likely find on buying party membership is you'll be inundated with fundraising emails and perhaps calls. While it can be annoying, it's a reality in party operations. Money is the lifeblood of a political party and there is no prospect list hotter to work on than the party membership list. You can always delete emails soliciting contributions and politely decline to donate when fundraisers call, but keep in mind many of those contacting you will be party volunteers, so be patient with them.

If you do want to donate, the tax credits are substantial. In Alberta, you'll get a 75 percent tax credit for contributions up to $200. That means a $200 contribution will only cost you $50, in the long run. If nothing else, politicians always make it easy for Canadians to fund their parties. Check local rules on contributions to parties and candidates before acting. The regulations on maximums can be convoluted and confusing sometimes. Parties are constantly getting caught up in micro-scandals over ineligible contributions and related issues—easily avoided if provincial party contribution rules are checked first.

Active membership also means the party can inform you about events and activities. Opting for email notifications is the best way to stay up to date, even if the party abuses your inbox on occasion.

Party membership entitles you to more than just junk mail, of course. Members take part in everything from policy formulation, selecting party executives, and choosing leaders and election candidates. The process for all those selections varies from party to party, but in the end it all comes down to the members.

Now engage with your local party organization. Federal ridings have organizations called electoral district associations and those of provincial organizations are usually called constituency associations. They all tend to operate the same way.

A healthy functioning local association is essential for a party's success. If you've ever experienced an election campaign where the local candidate was a non-starter or even invisible, it's usually a sign of weak local organization.

With any decent party, local electoral associations are where the rubber hits the road. A well-organized local association will be responsible for selecting a local candidate, fundraising, preparing for the local election campaign, communicating with the central party, and selecting delegates for party conventions. These associations are often starved of active volunteers and participants, particularly between elections. Independence-minded people can and should dominate these groups and it won't take many people to do it.

Nuts and bolts

Once you've joined a party, seek out your local organization. A smaller party might not have one, but larger parties will almost always have some sort of organization in each electoral division. If the party website doesn't point you to a local organization, find related social media groups or forums so you can network with other local members. You might even have get involved and form your own local association. The legal requirement for the formation of a local association typically involves holding a meeting to appoint or elect a president and a treasurer; this is the bare minimum. Next a bank account can be set up—assuming the party has sanctioned the association—and the association can get rolling.

When an association is in place, it will usually operate as a micro version of the party itself. A board of directors will govern it. There will be several directors with roles ranging from VP membership to VP communications, along with directors at large. The association will have an annual general meeting (AGM) along with periodic meetings with the board. Getting on the board with the association is usually an easy task since there are often plenty of vacancies. Most boards are begging for volunteers.

The local association should be governed by a set of bylaws. Those bylaws are created by the party and standardized. If you're planning to be an active member of the association, be sure to get a copy of the bylaws and read them. They might be a bit dry, but they can save a lot of grief by guiding resolution to conflicts within an organization.

If you do choose to serve on the board of an electoral association, you will need patience. Committees can be tedious things and you have to accept that not every vote will go your way. Compromise and cooperation are essential and while you might have differing views on some policies, you are all on the same team in a committee situation. Avoid the temptation to stomp out of the room when a meeting goes badly. Many of the meetings can be enjoyable, too. They're often held in pubs and when the formal needs of the association are addressed, the group can have some productive discourse and get to know one another.

Associations will often form subcommittees. Join one—or more—dedicated to the activities that interest you, or form one if they're absent.

If a party is large, it will have some form of delegate system for their AGMs. Each constituency will send a fixed number of delegates. They'll vote on behalf of their association on business such as party policy and constitutional amendments. They'll also vote for members of the central party's executive committee. Some parties select their leader through the delegate system. If you want to attend the larger central party meetings, your path to these meetings runs through the local association. In smaller parties they'll often allow any member to attend a convention for a fee. Fees usually range from $60 to $600 for a weekend.

It generally isn't difficult to become a delegate for your constituency. If you're already actively involved in your constituency board or on committees, your chances of being selected as a delegate for a party convention are pretty good.

If you have the means and the motivation, aim to become a delegate for party assemblies. This is how independence-leaning leaders and policies can be selected and embedded in the party.

Members within their local constituency generally select candidates for elections. The selection process is called a nomination and the party sets the rules. It's imperative independence advocates take part in these nominations and work to ensure independence-minded candidates are selected.

In small parties, many if not most of the candidate spots will be filled by acclamation. That means only one person applied or qualified for the job and was selected by default. In larger parties, nomination races are very competitive and involve several candidates.

Candidate nomination races are excellent constituency-building exercises. Candidates and volunteers can spend weeks or even months knocking on doors for the party selling memberships. This helps raise funds and builds interest and expands the membership base in the area. Nomination contests can also bring out the worst in partisan politics. A dirty nomination race can shatter a constituency, and party interference in a nomination race can foster distrust between local organizations and the central party, resulting in unwelcome setbacks.

Nomination races are great proving grounds for prospective election candidates. Candidates' extreme tendencies and dirty secrets—if they exist—tend to get exposed during these internal nomination races. Lazy or abrasive candidates will wash out while hard-working, personable candidates will tend to prevail. It's like a test run for the general election and helps increase the local organization's chance of fielding a successful candidate.

Nomination contests offer good training opportunities for volunteers. In many cases, nomination race campaign principles are the same ones in place when an election campaign begins.

In most parties, the nomination process starts with the formation within the constituency association of a local nominating committee. This committee oversees the nomination process and interviews prospective candidates. It provides the first level of vetting, and while the committee should avoid disallowing candidates whenever possible, they will if they think a candidate might damage the party's interests or reputation.

Nomination committees are often where some of the worst race meddling happens. While those committees are usually populated by well-meaning volunteers, they're worth keeping an eye on in case a corrupted element slips in. If a person or group wants to rig a nomination, they'll often begin with the committee. If you plan to run for a nomination or be active in another person's nomination campaign, you should not be on the nominating committee.

Once past the application stage and assuming a nominee candidate has been accepted, it's then simply a matter of paying a deposit and getting to work. Deposits can vary. Some are held as bonds for good campaign behaviour while others exist to ensure candidates are serious about their run. Some are non-refundable.

In a nomination race, selling memberships is everything. Winning the support of existing members is important, but it tends to be the candidate who sells the most new memberships who wins the race. There will be a deadline for membership sales and a cut-off point when new members won't be able to vote in the race. Race candidates should check the rules very carefully to avoid disqualification. Many parties have rules in place to ensure every new member pays their own fee and signs off on their own application. This is done to avoid bulk buying of memberships for people without their consent. Yes, it happens.

On that note, when taking part in nomination races, keep it clean. Check the rules carefully and follow them. Scrutinize the competing candidates, but avoid attacking them. Always remember this is an internal race—you'll all be back on the same team when it's over. Getting personal will only divide internal support and weaken your constituency's chances when it's time to prepare for an election.

The next most important thing after selling memberships is getting members out to vote once nomination day arrives. Many people who are sold memberships during nomination races are only lightly committed to the party or candidate. If they're not contacted and encouraged—nagged perhaps—to get out to vote, many of them won't. Nomination races are easy to forget. They're not in the news and it is up to each candidate's team to make sure their supporters come out and vote for them.

Membership lists are usually shared with every candidate before nomination day. There will be a period in the run-up to the vote when every candidate reaches out to each member no matter who sold the membership. Bear in mind membership-to-vote conversion rates for in these kinds of races are dismal. Most new members will vote for the candidate who sold them the membership. While no member should be ignored in a nomination race, a candidate and their team should remain primarily focused on selling their own memberships and getting those members to the polls on voting day. A lot of energy can be wasted trying to convert members who will never budge.

If there are more than two candidates on nomination day, there are a number of ways to find a single candidate with majority support. If nobody gets over 50 percent on the first ballot, there might be an immediate runoff vote with the top candidates, or one scheduled for a later date. Ballots might have been ranked in a way that means selection can be done all in one shot. It really depends on the party and again demonstrates why it's so important to understand your local rules.

People power

As a member, *you* can influence the party policy platform. All parties are important, but as an independence supporter, there's one policy more important than all of them; every province must have a policy for citizen-initiated, binding referendums. Their being both binding and citizen-initiated is essential. Within the legislation, the bar to invoke a referendum has to be set at a reasonable level. This legislation takes the power out of the hands of the politicians and puts it into the hands of the people where it belongs. It makes independence possible without an overtly independence-supporting government in power.

Most parties require that policy submissions for central party consideration—at a general convention or policy convention—come from constituency associations rather than individuals. This allows for a limited and manageable number of policy submissions and a degree of policy vetting before they reach the floor. Arm-twisting and other unprincipled political behaviours on policy formulation are not uncommon. The more informed and active members are in the process, the more equipped they are to fend off inside attempts to derail new policies. Undoubtedly, staffers and some politicians will attempt to hijack the process and disable the ability to invoke referendums. Watch out for them and know what steps are available to stop them.

It is a tough process. While a party might want to give members as much ability as possible to take part in policy determination, it just isn't feasible to accommodate every request. Don't get into the weeds with pet issues and prescriptive policies. Find the independence-related policies—or create them—and work to keep them on top and in focus for the party, otherwise they can be lost in the mix.

When I was VP of policy for the Wildrose Party, we once had no fewer than 600 policy submissions prior to a convention. When our party was small, the bar of having just five members endorsing a policy to get it put on the order paper wasn't a problem. When the party grew, we were overwhelmed with submissions. Policy proposals varied from long and prescriptive to those that were outright insane. We couldn't review them all at a general meeting. We had to pare down submissions to a few dozen and, predictably, some people whose policies hadn't made the cut were furious. Consequently, we developed a system of constituency-based policy formulation.

Policy—the life and death of a party

Parties are defined by their policies. Policies reflect the direction of the party membership and the ideology of the party itself. That said, party policies are overrated in many ways. At best, policies serve as a general guide for elected caucus members at provincial *and* federal level. Elected officials are not duty bound to promote or support party policy in any formal way. In the legislature and in Parliament, political representatives will often vote contrary to their own party policies. It might happen if a vote was based on constituency needs, leader's orders, or their own views—views that might not have aligned with party policy at the time.

Voters rarely read a party's policy set, but it's almost always pored over by party opponents, and the media will also scrutinize it. No party wins elections simply by virtue of their policy set, but they can certainly lose an election by it, especially if something within it is considered extreme. This is an important reason why any party's referendum-based policy ought not to be definitive.

We need the referendum and we need the public debate on independence, but we don't need to have it during the throes of a general election when it will become a distraction rather than remain the goal. A party can only campaign on so many fronts. Work hard on the process to enable a referendum. When that time comes, the independence discussion can truly begin. Here we're again reminded of the importance of patience.

Policies are important and must be taken seriously but they shouldn't be hills to die on. Keep it simple and work strategically.

The political machine

If you're active in your party, the next level beyond local organization is its convention. Party conventions and conferences are where the most important decisions about a party's direction are made, at least from a member's standpoint. The provincial executive committee is usually chosen at conventions. The most important policy deliberations take place there. In parties where delegates choose the leader, it happens at a convention. If you truly want to take part in the higher echelons of party management, you will need to attend these gatherings.

Conferences have social and procedural aspects. They're great places for active members to socialize, network, and bond. There will usually be a cocktail reception and often people in contention for executive positions within the party will have hospitality suites providing complimentary liquor. Hospitality suites are where party members can gain candid insight into its party main players since they tend to let their hair down after a few drinks and shed some inhibitions. Many can overindulge and make fools of themselves at these events, too. Take part in and enjoy these social activities. They're productive and can offer some excellent opportunities for one-on-one discussions with other party members.

Conventions can be fun and informative, but remember your purpose there. You'll want to be able to recall beneficial interactions. If you sip too much, you might do something you'll regret. That advice stands for all social events, and if you have serious political aspirations, you must be especially careful.

Some have to learn the hard way. About fifteen years ago, I drank far too much at one gathering while in a hospitality suite and decided to lay into one political activist I didn't much care for. I was belligerent and loud. It's not a moment I'm proud of. The incident has been forgotten by most, thankfully. If I were to pull such a stunt today, it would doubtless be recorded by more than one person and posted immediately to social media, possibly with devastating consequences for me and any party I might be allied to. It was an important lesson and one I'm glad to have learned early on.

If you've ever worked in any volunteer setting, you'll know a tiny minority within any organization does the lion's share of the work. Political parties are no different. While every member is indeed important, only a small number take an active role. Party conferences are where you can meet and get to know those people who make a real difference in politics rather than just talk about doing it. They're the people we need when a referendum campaign rolls out. Political conferences are ideal opportunities to build productive relationships.

During the day, provincial candidates for the executive committee (EC) will deliver their pitches. Voting usually takes place later on and results are announced at the conference's end. When voting for an EC candidate, choose level-headed, patient, and rational supporters of independence.

The EC serves as the conduit between members and the party leader's office. If the EC is dysfunctional, a disconnection between the leadership and its members is inevitable. If a leader isn't in touch with his or her party members, they won't be winning elections. The selection of EC members is an important task. When I was on the board with the Wildrose Party, at times we had a prickly relationship with our then leader, Danielle Smith. The party's constitution put a lot of power into the hands of the board and Smith chafed under it a bit. Perhaps the party constitution needed improvement, or perhaps it didn't. One thing I can say for sure is the bickering between the leader and the EC wasted a lot of time and squandered party unity. Compromise and cooperation can be tough, but they are essential to those party roles.

If you think you can serve on a party's EC, check the party constitution for the requirements to pursue a spot well before the next scheduled conference. In a large party, those positions are hotly contested, and you will want to start campaigning early for the role. It is, however, a lot of work to secure those unpaid and often thankless positions. If you really want to influence internal party direction, that's where you need to be.

Conferences will often hold breakout sessions and seminars. These are opportunities for learning you shouldn't pass up, even if some sessions might sound a little dull. You'll get a chance to hear candid presentations from party insiders and gain insight and training. Session topics can cover everything from successful social media campaigning to managing local election campaigns.

Party policy and constitutional proposals and amendments will usually be discussed and decided at conferences. Participation is tedious sometimes, but rewarding. Be sure to support policies that encourage provincial autonomy while opposing policies that pull the province closer to the federal government. Your support for or opposition to policies can come in the form of your vote, taking to the microphone to speak at meetings, and by campaigning one-on-one with folks during coffee breaks. Be on the lookout to block policies that could potentially cause scandal down the road. Try to view policy through the eyes of an undecided voter rather than use your own less objective frame of reference.

Conventions can be fun and productive, get to them if you can. If independence supporters don't dominate party gatherings, the party likely won't be supportive of independence.

When it comes to party politics, a general election is the Superbowl. It's what members spend years preparing for. It's the culmination of all party events, fundraisers, and organization. Take part in the campaign whether or not your preferred party or candidate has a realistic chance of winning a seat.

I don't want to go too deeply into the details of campaign management and strategy, there are countless books already written on the subject by more experienced campaigners than me. I do want to stress the importance of getting involved in the campaign itself, though. There is no better way to get that kind of training than to volunteer in an election campaign.

Election campaigns always need more volunteers. Find out who is running your preferred campaign and put your name forward. Organizers will likely get back to you right away. If they don't, it might be a sign that is not the campaign for you.

In some ways, volunteers are more important than donors. A genuine volunteer showing up at a door during a campaign is worth hundreds of glossy brochures and expensive ads. Any good campaign will be focused heavily on door knocking and voter identification. Putting a candidate face-to-face with a prospective voter is the best way to win support. Face-to-face with a volunteer comes next. A real-time phone call from a volunteer is valuable, too, while recorded calls are less likely to hit the spot. Honest, in-person communications with voters will always be the most effective way to win support. It takes a small army of volunteers to do that effectively.

Many people shy away from door knocking and phone work. A campaign is an ideal time to step out of your comfort zone and try it out. It's like most things; once you do it for a while, it becomes easy. Developing the ability to approach people with confidence and speak with them is a valuable life skill in general, never mind during elections.

If you start direct campaigning, you will encounter hostile people who viscerally oppose your efforts. Most of us don't like conflict and the experience can be off-putting. You'll have to learn to let those experiences slide off you, and experience is the best way to practice. Most people you encounter while campaigning will be polite and easygoing. Don't let the jerk minority stop you taking part.

And don't wear yourself out. If a volunteer coordinator realizes you are an eager worker, they will schedule you in so heavily you'll forget what your paying job was. Keeping the campaign fun is important. There will be breaks, rallies, and gatherings for drinks and pizza after campaign events. They really can be a great time and it makes the whole experience much more enjoyable—it doesn't have to be a grind. Make time for yourself.

Network with active and experienced campaigners. What better place to meet your local political movers and shakers than in a local campaign office?

If you really can't get with the door knocking thing, there are still plenty of opportunities to help: office management, sign placement, flyer dropping, to name a few. The tasks are plentiful. Find out what suits you best.

Many door knockers become confused when they're sent out to identify voters. They're coached to find out how a person plans to vote without getting into a back-and-forth. It is all part of a strategy called "get out the vote" (GOTV) and it's a critically important task. During an election campaign, the role of winning the hearts and minds of voters falls mostly into the hands of the central party. Local campaigns will be tasked with finding voters who are already onside, or almost onside. There just won't be time to have volunteers chat at every doorstep trying to win voters. A talkative doorknocker could spend an entire day working just a couple of city blocks.

In a close race, the campaign that gets the most supporters to the polls on Election Day will be the one that prevails. Voter turnout is low at the best of times and voters must be reminded consistently to cast their ballot. Be careful not to encourage *opposing* voters, however. This is why it's essential to first identify party supporters and prompt them exclusively.

When a volunteer finds a supportive voter while door knocking, they will record it and it will go into the campaign database. Once the polling stations open, the GOTV campaign begins, and volunteers contact supporters to encourage them to vote. This is a busy time for everyone. No vote can be taken for granted when election outcomes can be won and lost on very narrow margins. Don't feel your personal skills are being wasted when tasked with voter ID work. It's important and the information you gather empowers the campaign.

On Election Day, volunteers will be tasked with scrutineering. Campaigns are allowed to designate people to attend the polling stations from the time the ballot boxes are sealed in the morning right until the counting is finished. It can be a dull task, but it's important. This is how vote rigging is prevented. It's pretty tough to stuff a ballot box or intimidate voters when representatives from every party are present and watching. I know a lot of people don't trust the process, but for the most part in Canada, elections are very well monitored and are not rigged, even if we sometimes don't like the outcome. Spending a day or even a few hours as a scrutineer will reveal how transparent the process actually is.

You can even have some very interesting experiences when scrutineering. I will share one example.

In 2006, I was working on an energy exploration project in Inuvik in the Northwest Territories. I was processing ground-penetrating radar data for data mapping. The job only took me a few hours a day. I had a lot of spare time so I volunteered for the local CPC candidate in the general election. He was based in the south in Yellowknife so only had time to appear in Inuvik once. I had the job of meeting people in nearby communities like Tuktoyaktuk and Aklavik on his behalf as well as other campaign tasks.

I had volunteered to take the first shift scrutineering on Election Day since most of my data processing work was the evening. I saw a broad mix of voters file into the gymnasium greeted by several translators. I rarely found anyone who couldn't speak English up there, but Cree, Dene, and Inuktitut were common first languages and Elections Canada wanted to ensure everyone was accommodated.

Those manning the tables at the polling station had been hired and trained to work the one day. Scrutineering is an easy task, but can be a dull one and it's a *long* day. Before I left my shift in the afternoon, many had been complaining about how bored they were.

I closely watched the election results as they were posted that evening. I wanted to see if my efforts had moved the needle at all. While the entire country had posted their local polling station results on the Elections Canada website, by the time I'd gone to bed, Inuvik still hadn't posted theirs. They were eventually published at 5am.

I later learned that one hour after my shift was over, three-quarters of those hired to work in the polling station declared their job too boring and walked out. The polling station electoral officer was put in a tough spot. He took the unusual step of hiring the scrutineers on the spot to cover the absences. He got them to take the oath and he put them to work to get the job done. Untrained for the task, they did the best they could, but the voting lineups grew long. They closed the poll late and with only a handful of volunteers to count the ballots, they were up late into the night. The whole experience was pretty unique.

The story illustrates how even the dullest of electoral tasks can suddenly become very interesting and how participation in politics leads to some memorable times. Campaigns can be fun and offer unpredictable experiences and oftentimes you'll get a free lunch thrown in.

The skills and relationships developed during an election campaign can and should be carried over into a referendum campaign—the tactics and strategies are all the same, except you'll be selling a concept rather than party policies.

It will be hard to coordinate a successful referendum campaign without experienced boots on the ground and for this, elections offer the best training. Political parties alone aren't what will bring westerners to independence, but we won't achieve independence without party collaboration.

It's going to take a multifactor approach to build the winning conditions necessary to achieve and win an independence referendum. Parties are a part of every one of those steps and we need to be involved in them.

Chapter 10

LET'S LEARN FROM QUEBEC

Rather than be infuriated with Quebec, we need to learn from them. If possible, we should consider alliances with their independence movements. Quebec's independence movement goes all the way back to 1867 when Canada was formed. It never really blossomed into a strong political force until the 1960s, but it has always existed.

Quebecers have made many mistakes. Some of their secessionists have committed atrocious acts in their pursuit of independence. We never want to emulate the terrorism of the murderous Front de Libération du Québec and we don't want to embrace the bigotry of their language protection policies. We need to look at these efforts with an eye to ensure we don't take the same route. However, we can see where they've had their successes and can emulate those efforts.

Quebec stands up for its own interests without apology. They know their province is heavily favoured within Confederation and of course they don't care. They're not driven by a sense of fairness, they're driven by self-interest. They are not hostile to the rest of Canada in any way. They simply have no interest in it. Neither does the West need to hold any region of Canada in contempt. We should just stop concerning ourselves with what other Canadians think.

So, what *does* make Quebec powerful on the national scene? Is it that they have Members of Parliament in the federal governing party? Or is it because they have many Bloc Québécois MPs who speak only on issues that impact Quebec? The only way the main parties can potentially dislodge Bloc members is to address the regional issues they would otherwise prefer to ignore.

The West was never better represented than when it had the Reform Party in Parliament. Conservative Party members were forced to pay attention to the West and the Liberal government even managed to balance the budget under a fierce Reform Party in Opposition. How well was the West treated when Brian Mulroney was in power? How many structural changes did Harper make or even try to make to address regional imbalances while he was prime minister? Having a regionally focused party is in the West's best interest even if that party isn't overtly in favour of independence. We figured this out decades ago. Has that lesson been lost?

Quebec's political parties don't wear their independence objectives on their sleeves. The Parti Québécois and Bloc Québécois make it clear the interests of Quebec are paramount, and there's little doubt the majority of their members holds sovereigntist ideologies. Their efforts to ensure their independence goals don't eclipse all other policy goals are noteworthy. It allows them to grow and widen their appeal across a much broader portion of the electorate. Watch while they continue to build the foundation for a successful vote for independence in a future referendum.

Quebec has never hesitated to distance itself from Ottawa's control. Some westerners get riled up when pointing out how Quebec refused to sign the Constitution Act in 1982. Why should we be upset? Quebec's former premier René Lévesque didn't believe Trudeau was offering a good deal for Quebec at the time, so he told Trudeau to go to hell. Good for him. Quebec stood its ground and should be applauded rather than condemned.

Quebec has its own police force and its own pension plan, and they collect their own income taxes. They even call their provincial legislature the "National Assembly" in defiance of their being part of a larger nation.

Every move Quebec makes is an incremental effort to make their province more independent within Canada with the goal of eventually making it an independent nation altogether. Why aren't *we* doing this?

Some of it's due to our own prejudices—prejudice we must overcome. We have to set aside our annoyance at how Quebec has gamed the system and consider what we can learn from them.

When I was leader of the Alberta Independence Party, I sat down and talked to Richard Marceau who was at the time a Member of Parliament with the Bloc Québécois. It was a very enlightening meeting. At least one thing I learned was that those who strive for Quebec's independence have a genuine and sincere motivation, and they want out. Theirs is not a movement that issues threats simply to get their way on specific policies.

The Quebec independence movement has been actively working for decades and while they haven't achieved independence yet, they've come within one percent of a successful vote in a secession referendum and they're still working towards winning this referendum in the future. They have oceans of experience we can draw upon and many of them would be more than happy to share that experience with us. We have more goals in common with the Québécois than many people think. Our western independence-focused movements need to build a respectful and collaborative relationship with those of the Québécois. We have much to learn from them. If you want to see the Laurentian Elite truly panicked, get independence movements in both the West and Quebec working cooperatively!

In my meeting with Marceau, I also learned the West ought to broaden its perspective. Quebecers aren't an enemy. They are victims of a broken system as much as we are. When news of our meeting went public, the backlash from many of our own party members was instant and furious. I had been judged a traitor for even sitting down with a Quebec MP. Some never forgave me for it.

Let's stop looking at Quebec as an enemy and consider their potential as an ally. We need to think more broadly and respond more creatively if we want to grow and evolve the independence movement.

If Quebec achieves independence, it will be the domino that sets others falling. Other provinces will soon follow. Likewise, if a western province were to secede first, Quebec would be hot on those heels. Canada's national unity is already fragile—a consequence of its broken system. Once one province secedes, it will be difficult to sustain a frail union.

We should be supporting Quebec's path to independence whenever possible so we're primed to cultivate a productive and mutually supportive relationship, post-independence. It would serve us well. Both Quebec and the West would clearly be happier as independent entities and we could develop close trading ties. When we sit at the negotiating table as independent nations—rather than competitors in a broken Confederation—the potential exists to forge great trade agreements.

If Quebec was no longer benefitting from equalization payments, they would be far more inclined to support ingoing oil and gas pipelines and the development of energy export terminals in the province. Many mutually beneficial agreements are possible if Ottawa is taken out of the equation. Yes, products would still have to cross Ontario to get to Quebec. Negotiations would likely be conducted with rationale and doubtless more successful if Ontario were bracketed by independent states.

The time to start building that relationship is right now. Set aside past grudges and look ahead.

Chapter 11

WHAT WILL INDEPENDENCE LOOK LIKE?

A clear vision of an independent west must be well established prior to a referendum. Defeat is assured if independence proponents are offering a great policy vacuum and no tangible concept of what a new state would look like. That said, if independence advocates get mired in speculation on the specifics of policy and paradigm, the vision will collapse under the weight of uncertainty. In order to be saleable, a vision must be accessible.

So how to present a post-independence scenario?

Let's begin by using positive language. We must always frame independence as a positive beginning rather than a questionable end. Yes, we should invest time pointing out the negative aspects of the current system, however we should always aim to balance that argument with all the redeeming qualities of full independence. This would be especially important in the context of an imminent referendum.

Don't get into the weeds with policies but be sure to highlight principles. Talk about protecting and entrenching inalienable individual rights such as the right to property, freedom of speech, mobility, and the sanctity of the individual. Talk about the empowerment of citizens through democratic reform and how a rejuvenated system can protect important freedoms not only now, but for generations. Rather than the means to an end, present western independence as an opportunity in and of itself. A newly independent west could create one of the most inspiring reimagined democratic systems in the world and set the example globally for nation states to follow. How often do citizens get a chance to help draft a brand-new system of governance?

There would be two central objectives for a new governing system—decentralized government and fiercely protected (truly) democratic rights. While I have already suggested avoiding the quagmire of a constitutional redesign, we need something we can explicitly cheer for in a potential new system. The Swiss government model is a good one to contemplate since it addresses so many of the problems that centralized systems of governance create. Government authority is decentralized, and individuals are empowered through referenda.

We will have the opportunity to create an entirely new system of government and we will need to be measured and cautious while creating it. Painful experience has shown us without doubt that an established political system is very difficult to change even when it no longer serves citizens' interests.

Ode to the Swiss

We need not reinvent the wheel for a new political model, we can learn from the mistakes and successes of other nations around the world. I contend the Swiss system of governance offers the best example, aspects of which we could confidently embrace with little risk or reservation. Its framework would eliminate many of the flaws that have led us in Canada to the brink of the dissolution of the Confederation.

Switzerland is a landlocked nation with limited natural resources. It's less than a tenth the size of Alberta and has four official languages. Despite its small size and diverse population, it boasts one of the oldest and most stable democracies in the world. It's also one of the wealthiest and most peaceful nations. They've empowered their citizens through a significantly decentralized system of governance distinguished by its consistent application of direct democracy. Switzerland entrusts all major decision making to its citizenry and history tells us Swiss citizens are fully capable of responding to that authority and power with wisdom and prudence. It's tough to argue an independent west would be any different.

Switzerland sees its government as a means to an end rather than an end in itself. That which governs best is that which governs least, and the expenditure record of Switzerland versus Canada is one example that illustrates this clearly. While Switzerland's government expenditure forms 36 percent of GDP, Canada's makes up 52 percent of GDP. The absence of a large intrusive government has allowed Switzerland to have a strong, diverse, and rich economy despite its geographical disadvantages.

Heavily centralized governance invariably leads to division, inequity, and strife. Switzerland is by far one of the most decentralized nations in the world as far as its government is concerned. Its federal government mandate is limited to the armed forces, currency, postal service, telecommunications, immigration, emigration, asylum requests, foreign relations, civil and criminal law, weights and measures, and customs duties. Everything else is managed by the local cantons, which are smaller localized units of government.

Despite its small geographical size, Switzerland is home to twenty-six cantons. Cantons enjoy tremendous independence. Each canton has its own constitution, legislature, executive, police, and courts. Taxation systems, health care systems, and official languages differ between the cantons. A Swiss canton population size can vary from 1.5 million people to 16,000 people. Despite this diversity and these disparities within Switzerland, the country maintains a strong national identity and pride. There are no serious independence movements, and the nation is stable. Paradoxically, the decentralization of power has resulted in a stronger sense of national unity.

Switzerland's federal government is unlikely to intrude on the authority of a canton. The federal government is bicameral. It has a 200-seat National Council and a 46-seat Council of States. Both Councils have identical powers and elected members govern both. Twenty of the cantons send two representative members to the Council of States while six half-cantons send a single member each. This is much like the equal, fully elected, and effective senate model the Reform Party pursued in the 1990s. When it comes to federal policy, this system keeps the more populous cantons from dominating the smaller ones. While there are still certainly some heated debates on some policy issues within the federal houses, compromise is essential.

Another hallmark of the Swiss system is its foundation of direct democracy. From the canton level to the federal level, referendums play a huge role. The Swiss go to the polls about four times each year to vote on various issues as well as to elect their officials. There are three types of referendum in Switzerland: popular initiative, mandatory, and optional.

Popular initiative referendums apply to amendments or additions to the nation's constitution. They are initiated when a minimum 100,000 citizens in support of a proposal sign its petition within eighteen months. Meeting the requirement to initiate a referendum is achievable yet the bar is not set so low as to encourage constant referendum questions on petty issues. Compare that to Alberta's ludicrous requirement of nearly 600,000 signatures within a ninety-day period to initiate a referendum. That's not direct democracy—it's an insult to it.

In Switzerland, mandatory referendums are triggered when its parliament proposes any change to its constitution. The requirement for those referendums truly symbolizes the Swiss philosophy that the will of its citizens should supersede that of the government. The government cannot make constitutional changes without seeking citizens' permission and approval—the state serves the people rather than the other way around.

An optional referendum allows the population to demand that any bill approved by the Federal Assembly be put to a nationwide vote. To initiate an optional referendum, 50,000 signatures are required within 100 days of the publication of the new legislation. Eight cantons can also submit a proposal and initiate a referendum on any proposed federal law.

Despite how relatively easy it is to initiate them in Switzerland, the nation isn't crippled by constant and frivolous referendums. Citizens for the most part treat their system with respect. We must conclude that when the population is empowered with a direct part in the nation's governance, they do a damn good job of it.

The Swiss system isn't perfect by any means, but no system is or ever will be. As proponents of western independence, we will be asked what kind of system we would like to see established, post-secession. It's a fair question and we will need to be able to answer confidently and with a convincing rationale. Perhaps someone will one day create an entirely unique and outstanding model that can be applied in the event of independence. In the meantime, Switzerland provides us a useful example of a successful, citizen-driven democratic model of governance that has an undeniable record of success.

Deconstruction and refederation

Western independence could conceivably offer the opportunity of a revised Canadian federation. A positive independence vote could lead to negotiations and the creation of a new agreement between the regions and provinces of Canada. Only the secession of a Canadian province from the Confederation will create the motivation to reform Canada's Constitution. Still, we might have to rule out a new agreement, post-secession. Perhaps the environment will not be conducive to a new agreement, but it's a scenario we shouldn't rule out. Canada as a federation doesn't necessarily need to end. It just needs a new contract.

Back in 2001, I had an excellent conversation with the late Ted Byfield on a radio show he had on Shine FM. Byfield spoke about a concept he called "refederation." He had written about it on several occasions in the *Alberta Report*, a magazine he published at the time. The concept is pretty straightforward: Canada can exist as a nation, but it would have to be torn down and rebuilt first.

We have to get out of the current Confederation in order to pursue a "refederation" under a new constitution. The only way to get out of the current form of confederation is for one or more provinces to secede. Then we could potentially negotiate as a nation an entirely new set of terms that would be practical while at the same time respect regional autonomy.

For some people, this concept might take the sting out of a sense of irrevocability associated with provincial secession. It offers a path for those who still feel we can and should maintain a nation that reaches from the Pacific to the Atlantic. Canada could continue to exist while the system gets a rebuild.

In a post-secession scenario, it would take a while for things to settle down before any productive discourse could begin on the potential of reuniting as a confederation. There will be some raw emotions and there will also be many who don't want to see the Confederation return in any form. If enough folks in the West and the East are receptive to a new deal, refederation is a concept that shouldn't be dismissed.

This is a helpful topic for discussion when speaking to people who are still on the fence about independence. Provincial secession doesn't have to spell the end of Canada and it could form a new chapter in a longer history of our nation. It must never be forgotten that even if the intent is to rebuild Canada in the long run, it's essential the Confederation be dismantled first. It can only happen through provincial secession. We've tried and failed too many times to fix the system from within.

Notes from the borderline

There has always been a subgroup among western independence supporters who want the West to join the United States in one way or another. Some propose individual provinces pursue US statehood. Others support the concept of Cascadia—a new nation comprising a number of northwestern US states and western Canadian provinces. We need to avoid these discussions in the context of the pursuit of western independence. They distract from and dilute the aims of the movement when we need to remain focused on the goal of breaking provinces free from Confederation. As long as provinces are still a part of Canada, the discussion remains open to debate.

People make several assumptions when speaking about a union with the US. The biggest assumption is that the Americans even *want* us to join us in the first place. The US has never shown any interest in expansionism or the expropriation of land from its neighbours. It is presumptuous to believe they'd be interested in subsuming one or more Canadian provinces, now or at all.

Many independence supporters have no interest in the idea of joining the US. We would be dividing our already limited support in proposing the concept. Achieving a tipping point of support for western independence is already a mammoth task.

The argument about a union with the US may or may not have merit, but these discussions cannot take place in earnest until at least one or more provinces has already voted to secede. I don't think any newly emancipated region would be remotely interested in becoming small fish in an even bigger pond than the one left behind. We mustn't distract from our base objectives with frivolous debates like this, now or at any time during our independence campaign.

While provinces one-by-one will have to vote in their own independence referendums, would they all form independent nations, or join in a single unified region?

This is where it gets complicated. Every province must first vote on its own fate. Any vote on independence has the potential for new alliances or agreements with other provinces, but the waters can't be muddied too much with the discussion on the variables, or a positive vote in a referendum will never happen. That said, it must be understood that independence *could* mean the creation of a new nation and that it might be a union with other, newly independent provinces.

When any one province is nearing the point of a referendum win for independence, it must be assumed that Canadian unity generally is at low ebb and that other provinces might also be on the brink of voting for independence.

Independence movements in all provinces should at least be to be open to discussion on the topic of post-secession relationship. Commitment to formal plans is not yet necessary.

The idea that independent provinces come together as a new nation is acceptable only if its principal basis is the decentralization of power. Federation is achievable, but it has to be under a new system.

We simply must discuss what an independent west will look like. We cannot, however, allow that discourse to descend into a series of hypothetical scenarios and what-abouts. The discussion on the issue has to remain broad and positive. If we go down the rabbit hole of variables, people will struggle to visualize the appeal of an independent west and they won't vote in favour. Stay positive and keep your vision broad and engaging when you present your argument.

Conclusion

Canada's system of Confederation is defective and without hope of repair. The dissolution of the federation is inevitable. The only question is how and when it will happen. As long as independence movements continue with the same old tried and failed strategies and continue to flounder, western independence will be delayed. Canada's flawed system will continue to damage the West's economic prosperity and the well being of its people. With a brand-new approach focused on the individual's role in the dissemination of ideas for independence, we can accelerate our passage towards it and ensure a positive transition instead of having to endure a tumultuous and ugly divorce.

We can create the necessary environment for western independence by taking on the task of advocacy as an army of individuals. We have to accept that ours is the responsibility of ambassadorship. We can foster a desire for western independence one convert at a time. Our confident and educated endorsement and promotion of our ideas will create new supporters more effectively than any advocacy group or political party. A carefully crafted viewpoint from a family member, colleague, friend, or neighbour will have far more influence and impact than that of an academic or professional politico.

Remember to convey your message in the spirit of a dedicated advocate rather than that of a careless fanatic.

The same old flawed arguments against independence have been used for decades. Those arguments have, however, been effective because we simply haven't had salient and consistent counterpoints at the ready to rebut them. We have the ability to defang the common arguments made against western independence only as long we're ready to respond to them with well-prepared and assertive rebuttals.

Presently, we are compelled to labour under the current system, and we are continually hamstrung by it. Thanks to Quebec's past efforts on independence, the passing of the Clarity Act gives us the mechanism to escape it entirely. Attempted reformation of our contemporary political model via its own system and framework will consistently result in failure and demoralization.

With a citizen-initiated referendum, we can use the rules created within Confederation to lawfully disentangle ourselves from it. Our collective and individual focus must hold fast to the two primary goals of realizing independence: acquiring citizen powers to initiate binding referendums and the creation of the winning conditions for secession when an independence referendum comes.

Political parties will have an essential contribution to make in the quest for western independence. We need their people power and organizational skills in the battle for the prerequisite referendum legislation. Let's also quit spawning parties with independence as a primary mandate. No single-issue independence party has ever been viable in the West, and none ever will be. The secession movement must be decentralized and cannot be tied to any single partisan entity. Political party know-how will allow us to participate effectively on the inside and will profoundly influence parties' mandates. We can no longer sit on the sidelines and let federalists continue to dominate party politics and direction.

Eventually, an independence referendum will be necessary in every western province. Those referendums can only be won if independence advocates are prepared, and they campaign effectively. When the rubber hits the road and campaign time arrives, we must be eager and energized to participate full throttle.

Participation in municipal, provincial, and federal election campaigns will help train and prepare advocates for constructive and rewarding referendum campaigns. We must not allow those opportunities to pass us by, even if partisan politics can seem frustrating and pointless at times.

The mainstream media will oppose the movement, but social media gives us the means to bypass those traditional gatekeepers to information. Positive, pro-independence messaging can dominate discussion if enough sensible voices are on top of the conversation.

There will be some irrational, extreme and offensive voices purporting to speak for the independence movement. We can never get rid of them all, but we can overwhelm them by sheer weight of numbers and keep the rational individuals on top of the dialogue and messaging. This way, the crazies can be called out and sidelined before they get a chance to derail the movement.

Western independence isn't an impossible aspiration. It's truly within our grasp and the path to it is realistic and navigable. It's a simple question of adjusting our approach to the challenge and maintaining a single-minded determination to usher in an independent west.

Quit wasting precious time waiting for some other person or group to take care of this for you. Stop waiting for a messiah to take the lead. Take up the mantle for yourself and strive to build the foundation for the western independence we all need. After all, it's asked, "If not us, then who? If not now, then when?"

Thousands of motivated individuals acting independently on shared and cherished goals will achieve what dozens of groups and political parties have so far failed to do. Together we can free the West.

Manufactured by Amazon.ca
Acheson, AB

13449865R00122